Grandpa's Hodgepodge and Potpourri

A book of miscellany

By

Joe Morris

TABLE OF CONTENTS

DEDICATION

This book is dedicated to all those who enjoy reading eclectic writings. Books can be fiction or non-fiction. They can be history or biography, science fiction or romance. What you will read here is a smorgasbord of ideas, plus idioms, quotes, statistics, and more. There is no flow in thought from one chapter to another. For readers who enjoy digesting one chapter at a time, this book is for you.

ACKNOWLEDGMENTS

Thank you to my wife, Linda, for patiently listening to some of the chapters in this book. Also, friends have encouraged me by showing interest in reading some chapters.

ABOUT THE AUTHOR

Joe was a 1973 graduate of the University of North Carolina at Chapel Hill with a Bachelor of Science degree in Business Administration. After college, he worked at a mortgage company for eighteen years before leaving to write. Returning to work full-time, he retired in 2023 after twenty-eight years at Wells Fargo. His first writings were not published, so this will be his first published book.

THINGAMAJIGS

Are there times in your life when you need to use a word but cannot think of it? You know what a thing looks like, how to use it, and where it is, but you cannot remember its name. No amount of racking your brain will give you the name. Finally, in frustration, you utter the words, "Please bring me that thingamajig. " (Other words that may be used include doohickey, whatchamacallit, doodad, etc.)

With our ever increasingly complicated, technological society, thingamajig has become a synonym for many new words (and old words) in our vocabulary. New words are coined constantly in medicine, politics, sports, and the legal profession. It is virtually impossible to learn all the latest additions to our increasingly expanded lexicon. Without knowing or not remembering the new word in a certain field, we may use it as a synonym for the words thingamajig, doohickey, or whatchamacallit. Hopefully, our synonym will be understood as we provide more details about the word that we need to use.

Thingamajig has become a vital part of my vocabulary. For years, even decades, it has been frustrating trying to remember the right word to use for something or in a certain situation. While I fumble around in my mind searching for the right word to use, someone may notice my frustration, they may understand what my search is for, and they may provide me with the correct word. Of course, I am thankful for their help, but it embarrasses me to show them my ignorance.

At my age, medicine seems to be the field where my ignorance expresses itself most clearly. New words in politics, sports, and the legal profession have me flummoxed, but new words for drugs and disease escalate a lot faster in my world. Thankfully, I'm on no drugs, only eye drops, so it's hard to carry on an intelligent conversation with others who go from drug to drug. When I can't think of the correct word for a medicine, whatchamacallit may be used. When the name of a sports team cannot be recalled, whatsthename can be expressed. If I can't remember the name of a tool, doodad will do. More details must be provided so the correct tool can be identified.

To limit my use of synonyms, it is helpful to eat foods that are good for the brain. I have read that green leafy vegetables, berries, nuts, and whole grains are good brain foods. For breakfast, I sometimes enjoy blueberries and bananas on oatmeal or Grape Nuts cereal. Walnuts as a snack help satisfy my need for brain food. As I age, good nutrition, good exercise, and plenty of sleep can help my cognitive abilities stay functional. But in situations where the correct word will just not come to mind, I can always use a synonym.

ONE-LINERS

Joe Morris: The criminal would have been hanged except for a hung jury.

Harry Callahan: Go ahead, make my day.

Winston Churchill: Success is the ability to go from one failure to another with no loss of enthusiasm.

Helen Keller: Life is either a daring adventure or nothing.

Oscar Wilde: Always forgive your enemies – nothing annoys them so much.

Yogi Berra: No one goes there anymore, it's too crowded.

Casey Stengel: You have to have a catcher, otherwise you will have a lot of passed balls.

Babe Ruth: Baseball was, is, and always will be the best game in the world to me.

Duffy Daugherty: I could have been a Rhodes Scholar, except for my grades.

Tom Landry: A champion is simply someone who did not give up when they wanted to.

Tony Adams: Play for the name on the front of the shirt, and they'll remember the name on the back.

Love Story: Love means never having to say you're sorry.

The Godfather Part II: Keep your friends close, but your enemies closer.

The Godfather: I'm going to make him an offer he can't refuse.

Jaws: You're gonna need a bigger boat.

The Wizard of Oz: There's no place like home.

Field of Dreams: If you build it, he will come.

Taxi Driver: You talkin' to me?

Good Will Hunting: How do you like them apples?

Star Wars: May the Force be with you.

Joe Morris: If the bread doesn't rise, that's the yeast of your problems.

Apollo 13: Houston, we have a problem.

Anonymous: When you're well, you have many desires, but when you're sick, you have only one.

Mark Twain: A successful marriage requires falling in love many times, always with the same person.

The Terminator: I'll be back.

Casablanca: Here's looking at you, kid.

Raiders of the Lost Ark: Why did it have to be Snakes?

A Few Good Men: You Can't Handle the Truth.

E. T. : E. T. , phone home.

Snow White: Magic Mirror on the wall, who is the fairest one of all?

Babe: That'll do, Pig. That'll do.

Frankenstein: It's alive! It's alive!

Wizard of Oz: Pay no attention to that man behind the curtain.

Terminator 2: Hasta la vista, baby.

Forrest Gump: Mama says, 'Stupid is as stupid does. '

Cool Hand Luke: What we've got here is a failure to communicate.

Dr. No: Bond, James Bond.

The Shining: Here's Johnny.

Airplane: I am serious. And don't call me Shirley.

MARRIAGE

Is there anything more important to our society today than marriage? You might say it is the glue that helps families stay together. One man. One woman. One couple. Two become one. Then the one becomes three, four, five as children are added to the family. Then the children grow up, find their mates, marry, and have their children, who are grandchildren to the one man and one woman. Marriages populate society as couples expand their families.

Increasing the population is only part of marriage. It fulfills the original mandate, "Be fruitful and multiply", but marriage involves so much more than having children. The husband and wife have responsibilities to manage, especially to each other. Ideally, opinions, personality differences, and individual tastes were worked out before the couple became one. Agree to disagree, be patient, and learn to enjoy new foods. It's a new world where loneliness is gone. (If you are lonely in marriage, that's a problem.) It is best to work out the problems that can be worked out before children are born.

If you experienced no major problems before having children, congratulations! If you had no major problems after having children, could I have your telephone number? Loneliness is not a problem for couples with children. Challenges accompany the children as they become part of the family. They must be taught their own responsibilities within the family. After learning to crawl, then walk, they must learn the alphabet and numbers. Reading, writing, and arithmetic then became part of their discipline. While these and other disciplines are being taught, children should socialize with other children. What they learn in their youth will be needed throughout their lives as they make decisions.

While teaching their children, each husband and wife must not neglect their own needs. The engagement period should have revealed some of each other's needs. As the years progress, as boys and girls become part of the family, more needs are manifested. The man needs recognition for something he has done. A woman needs confidence in the security provided by her husband. They may both bring home the bacon, or one may work while the other cares for the children. This is just one challenge that must be answered.

I've very briefly touched on marriage, with and without children. My concern now is the appearance of a marriage with no commitment. Commitment must be a vital part of marriage since ideal marriages last until the death of one of the parties. Considering that life continues through marriages, there should be a desire for each to continue together after they have married.

Why do people unite without commitment, without getting married? Many things said to each other before uniting are not fulfilled later. Domestic disputes are not fully resolved, and feelings are hurt beyond recovery. Maybe the couple was too young to marry, but they decided to hitch up anyway. Maybe they wanted an escape hatch, a way to get out of their union without going through a divorce and all the headaches involved with a dissolution. If the decision is made to marry, the couple should receive good counsel. A good marriage counselor can offer wisdom to the couple to help them make the right decision.

WRITING

There are many ways to communicate. Talking, body motions, pictures, and writing are just a few of the ways. Teaching, preaching, radio, television, and YouTube are channels for talking and using body motions. (You won't see body motions on the radio.). Images that talk are shown in pictures on television and YouTube. Writing is expressed through several mediums as you will read in this chapter.

One form of writing is through letters and cards. Letters are personal and reflect the personality of the writer. When several pages of material will be sent, a letter will probably be used rather than a card. For short notes, a card would be more appropriate. Cards are sent for birthdays, anniversaries, and holidays, such as Valentine's Day. St. Patrick's Day, Mother's Day. Father's Day, Thanksgiving, and Christmas. Cards may also have typed verses or phrases along with illustrations or pictures. They can express sympathy or joy, or any number of emotions. I have found that the Dollar Tree carries an excellent selection of cards at very reasonable prices. Letters and cards are the most intimate forms of writing.

Books spread their messages through printed pages. Types of books include biographies, fantasy, history, training manuals, and novels. Novels may be about science fiction, adventure, fantasy, romance, and horror. Writing books requires a lot of dedication, discipline, and hard work. In addition, a vivid imagination is needed to write a novel. Months or even years may pass before a book is ready to be published, so the author must be serious in their desire to finish writing the book.

For a quick note, one can text or email a message or send one on X. Text messages are generally limited to 160 characters, though multi-segment messages can be longer. Tweets on X can be up to 280 characters, though direct messages can be much longer. These two means of communication are much quicker to complete since they are typed rather than written. (I can certainly type faster than I can write.). They reach the recipient much sooner, also, since they are sent online. Because emails are sent online, they are also much quicker to communicate. Emails can be long, but they don't have that personal touch that one receives in a letter.

Closed Caption is shown on television to visualize in words or symbols what is audibly expressed on the screen. One would normally refrain from using Closed Caption because it interferes with the viewing. However, for the hearing impaired or in a noisy environment, it would be helpful to show what is said on television.

Monthly bills are paid by individuals, businesses, and other organizations, and are typically paid by cash, check, or online. A check used for payment requires the date, payee, amount (digitally and written out), and signature. This information can be typed or written on the check. Paying online may be less expensive since you do not need stamps to mail the check. My wife pays our bills online, but some other payments are paid by check and mailed. I prefer paying online to save some money, and it is easier than writing checks.

Writing is important. It is a discipline that everyone should employ and enjoy. Our tech-heavy society places more value on technology, where writing is not necessary, but we should not neglect writing. Technology loses the personal touch that writing expresses, so to keep our personalities, write those letters and cards. Pay your bills online or by check, but keep writing.

GAMBLING

Gamble. Risk. Chance. What is the chance that you will put a stake on some venture? Are you willing to take a risk to gain a reward? When does taking a risk become a gamble? Is every investment a gamble if the purpose of the investment is to increase the funds that are invested?

People invest every day. We invest our time, our money, our bodies, our minds, and our properties in our families, our businesses, our children's education, and in various ventures. The expectation is for a positive outcome: more money, a stronger, healthy body, or a mind disciplined to learn a profession or trade. The risk taken in the investment may be acceptable if the goal is worthy and would be enjoyable if the goal is reached. Is such an investment a gamble?

Suppose you buy some stock. You've done your homework, studied the market, analyzed the stock, and made your decision. You invest in the market hoping that your purchase will increase in value. You knew the risk involved, that the stock might lose value or even go broke, but you were willing to take the risk. By taking that risk, did you gamble? Would it make any difference if the stock went up or down?

Suppose someone else bought the same number of shares of the same stock at the same time. The decision was made on a whim – a guess that the stock would increase in value. No homework, no studying the market, no analysis. Would both stock purchases be investments, or would one be an investment and the other a gamble, or would both purchases be gambles? When does an investment become a gamble, or are all investments gambles? Both stock purchases involved the same risks, and both would achieve the same results.

Let's consider money "invested" in a game of chance at a casino. Whether it's a roulette wheel, a game of poker, or a slot machine, the money is spent on a gamble. These activities are clear examples of gambling. Money would be won or lost. Why are these games of chance considered gambles, but money spent buying stocks is considered an investment?

In a casino, when you pull the arm on a one-armed bandit, you take a chance on winning some money. It's all or nothing. When you lose, the money is gone. To continue playing the slot machine, you must insert more money. The same is true for the roulette wheel and other games of chance. It's all or nothing. You can say that playing these games is entertainment, and it is, but it is still gambling. If you don't have money you can afford to lose, don't gamble. The entertainment loses its excitement when you lose money you cannot afford to lose.

With an investment, you are seeking a long-term payout, unlike gambling, which is generally short-term. You invest and wait patiently while the investment grows, shrinks, and grows again. There is no growing and shrinking in gambling. When you lose, there is all shrinkage, and nothing is left to grow. If you gamble, please consider it entertainment. Don't expect a return on your money.

I hope you are wise when you spend money. (Know when to hold them, know when to fold them.) There are many pitfalls in society, with lots of requests for your money. Gambles are presented as investments, so you need good discernment to know the difference. You must decide whether to invest or to be entertained.

COMMON SENSE

Humans have five senses: seeing, hearing, touching, tasting, and smelling. We see with our eyes, hear with our ears, touch with our bodies, taste with our tongues, and smell with our noses. Some humans may have a sixth sense, which seems paranormal to those who don't have one. People with a sixth sense may sense an accident before it happens or know what people will say before they say it. It's as though they had a crystal ball to instruct them.

Along with the five senses and possible sixth sense, there is another sense that we call common sense. While the five senses come with your body, you are born with them; common sense is acquired from experience. People who have a hard time learning from their experiences may lack common sense at various times. There may or may not be a logical reason for common sense. It decides what is right or proper for an occasion.

Common sense is not passed down; it is not inherited. It can't be found in DNA or in a will. It is learned from life as you see others respond to situations and as you face circumstances where decisions must be made. For example, when it is raining, an umbrella is employed to keep dry. A driver's license is required whenever a vehicle is driven on the highway. A meat or vegetable with a suspicious smell is trashed rather than eaten. When a person becomes violently ill, they know to go to the emergency room or call 911.

People are constantly making decisions every day. These decisions may be based on knowledge or on guesswork. With good knowledge, there can be favorable outcomes. If the decisions are based on educated guesses about what to do, the outcomes probably won't be favorable. Common sense may be needed to ensure a good result.

An enemy to common sense is herd mentality. It is so much easier to let someone else make the tough decisions and then follow the crowd that acts on those decisions. With a leader who has shown wisdom in making decisions, it can be wise to follow his leadership. It takes good discernment to know who or what to follow. Do you follow someone's leadership or your conscience? Common sense can trump both.

Since common sense comes from experience, from the college of hard knocks, it is necessary to get involved in society to learn. Join clubs, be a part of teams (athletic, academic, or social teams), meet people as you walk, shop, and eat out. Engage in conversations and ask questions when you need an answer. You may embarrass yourself at times, but you will learn from your experience. In future similar situations, you will have the common sense to behave and respond correctly.

IN

You made it! You're in! The word 'in' has a good connotation. When you receive that acceptance letter from college, are accepted in the fraternity or sorority, or receive that promotion at work, you know you are 'in'. All the work of the past weeks, months, and years finally paid off. Your achievements were recognized, your accomplishments have been rewarded, and you are part of the team. You are 'in'.

Sometimes it is not good to be 'in'. To be in the wrong crowd, in the wrong job, or in the wrong place indicates that change is needed. The wrong crowd can get you into trouble. There can be trouble with your parents, your friends, or the police. The wrong job can be boring and not allow you to develop your talents or explore new opportunities. Being in the wrong place can be dangerous to your health or even your life. When you realize it is a bad situation, you must consider your options. Leaving the wrong crowd or wrong place should be obvious, though it may be hard to do. Leaving the wrong job should be done only if you have another job waiting. You want to be in the right crowd, right place, and right job.

Phrases with good meanings include in the know, in good hands, in good condition, and in a good situation. If you are 'in the know,' then you understand something or have some information that others may not have. You may be 'in good hands' in a hospital, on a guided tour, or at a well-respected university. A car, a house, or a piece of machinery may be 'in good condition' when it runs well or has no condition that needs immediate attention. With a good wife, a good job, or a good team, you are 'in a good situation'.

Many words begin with 'in' and some have a negative meaning. Inedible, inexact, inhumane, insincere, and insufficient are a few examples. Other words that begin with 'in' have a positive meaning, including incomparable, incorrupt, indispensable, inspire, and instruct.

We have considered the letters 'in' and phrases that include these letters. Now, let's consider a biblical phrase, 'In Christ. ' The apostle Paul uses this phrase several times in his epistles (New Testament books). The phrase appears in II Corinthians 5:17, 'If any man be in Christ, he is a new creature…' I Corinthians 15:22, For as in Adam all die, even so in Christ shall all be made alive…' and Ephesians 2:10, 'created in Christ Jesus unto good works'. Paul had extraordinary experiences as a Christian after his conversion on the road to Damascus. He never saw Jesus in the flesh, as did the other apostles, but was taught the scriptures by revelation. Thus, he learned that to be "In Christ" was to become alive as a new creature to do good works. To be "In Christ" is far better than to be with the 'in crowd'.

BACKACHES

Retirement can be exciting. After a life of working day after day, week after week, month after month, and year after year, one may anticipate freedom to enjoy life on his own time. Of course, there can be obstacles to that freedom; obstacles such as backaches. Life is not so enjoyable when one is constantly hurting.

I don't recall when my back first started hurting constantly. Perhaps it began in the eighth grade. My family's backyard had eight trees that I climbed occasionally. One cold morning before school, after climbing one tree, I lunged for the branch of another tree. My hands slipped and I fell on my back about seven feet to the ground. (Apparently, no one saw it, and no one was told about it.) The fall didn't prevent me from going to school, so maybe any injury incurred wasn't lasting.

Another time, I was alone walking on the property at my church. (Why do accidents happen to me when I'm alone?) There was a tree on the property with a branch about five feet off the ground. It extended several feet from the tree and parallel to the ground – a perfect opportunity for me to run and grab it. Unfortunately, the branch was rotten and broke when I grabbed it, causing me to fall on my back to the ground. Maybe my backache began then.

Instead of being caused by a fall, my backaches could be the result of a congenital condition. While taking piano lessons when I was twelve, an excruciating pain was felt in my lower back. The two incidents with trees may have simply aggravated the problem. Playing tackle football without pads might have contributed, also. With pain for years, I needed to find something or someone that would provide relief.

My decision to find relief was made when I was in my late twenties. Surgery or drugs to mask the pain were not considered. Chiropractic care was less intrusive with no long-term headaches (Why add another ache?) like a botched surgery or drug overdose would cause. I have enjoyed chiropractic care for over forty years now. That is one place where I don't mind, I even enjoy being "manipulated. " After years of chiropractic care, the chiropractor showed me an X-ray of the top of my back. There was a patch of white, maybe four inches by twelve inches, that he said was arthritis. Arthritis? Was my backache due to arthritis? Maybe the falls from the trees caused the arthritis.

That is my story on backaches, a pain I wish on no one. If you have backaches, whether you are retired or not, I hope you find the reason for the pain and get healed or get continual relief. There is help available. If you find relief or not, I hope you are looking forward to the day when there will be no more pain.

READING

Reading can be fun. It will take you to places you will never go, introduce you to people you will never meet, and provide you with information that you may never use. It can inform, infer, inspire, and instruct. Without reading, much of learning would be impossible. Learning by example or experience is useful, even necessary, but it cannot always replace the knowledge gained from reading.

I enjoy reading letters, magazines, books, and even some mail. Most of my mail is bills, ads, or solicitations for funds. I am required to pay my bills, encouraged to buy what is advertised, and asked to support some cause. Most of my book reading is for entertainment or enjoyment. Being retired, I don't read manuals, reference books, law reviews, or any material connected with a profession or trade. So what do I read?

Novels. Many good novels were written in the nineteenth century. Charles Dickens, Jules Verne, Victor Hugo, Thomas Hardy, and Charlotte Brontë were a few authors from that period. (I may be a grandpa, but these authors were not my contemporaries.). Some of their books include Oliver Twist, Twenty Thousand Leagues under the Sea, The Hunchback of Notre Dame, Tess of the d'Urbervilles, and Jane Eyre. Of these books, Jane Eyre was my favorite. Of these authors, the books of Jules Verne were the most exciting, and those of Thomas Hardy were the most depressing, especially Tess of the d'Urbervilles. I prefer novels with uplifting endings.

Short Stories. I don't read many short stories, but I really enjoy The Gift of the Magi by O Henry. Who can forget the surprise ending where a poor young couple's gifts to each other could not be enjoyed because of their sacrifices to buy the gifts? Edgar Allen Poe was a difficult read with foreboding, macabre plots, and dialogue. One of his stories seemed so weird that I did not finish reading it.

Poems. Poe also wrote poems. You will remember The Raven (Quoth the Raven, Nevermore). He also wrote Annabelle Lee and El Dorado. If you decide to read Poe's poems, take my advice and don't read right before bedtime. Poems by Robert Frost and Rudyard Kipling are a better choice for me. Stopping by Woods on a Snowy Evening and The Road Less Traveled are two poems by Frost. My favorite poem is "If" by Kipling. It starts with "If you can keep your head when all about you are losing them and blaming it on you. " This poem gives good advice to young men (and anyone, for that matter).

Eclectic Writings. For a variety of works, The Book of Virtues by William J Bennett is a good read. This book includes poems, speeches, short stories, and essays. The book calls itself a "how to" book for moral literacy. It has ten sections: Self-Discipline, Compassion, Responsibility, Friendship, Work, Courage, Perseverance, Honesty, Loyalty, and Faith. Each section has works designed to help the reader improve their moral character.

My journey through words has been challenging, tiring, exciting, and informative. It has been a much better experience than watching television or searching YouTube. If you have not developed a habit of good reading, I urge you to start. When you do, I think you will find it to be a rewarding experience.

EARLY RISERS

It is said that the early bird gets the worm. Though it is unclear when this phrase or proverb originated, it was well known by the latter seventeenth century. Perhaps an early riser (simply one who gets up early in the morning) saw a robin in their yard scratching for worms and finding one. That early riser may have been William Camden, who wrote a book of proverbs in 1605 that contained the phrase. It has become an effective phrase in our day as a stimulate to those who love to stay in bed but need to get up.

With our fast-paced society today, work schedules are 24/7 at hospitals, some fast-food restaurants, and operations that must be open around the clock. There are eight-hour shifts, ten-hour shifts, and twelve-hour shifts. With ubiquitous lighting, we are no longer limited to the sun's schedule. Work is continued around the clock.

Freeways are a good indication that lack of sunlight does not limit the time to travel. Headlights have replaced sunlight at night, so that freeways are busy all day and all night. (I recall when my wife and I were stuck in a Disney Resort because a hurricane was outside. The television showed I-4 with no traffic. Not a single car, truck, or bus!). When it is necessary to travel, time is not a limitation.

We can work around the clock and are not limited in our time for traveling. An early riser in the seventeenth century did not have these advantages, so rising early or getting ready to work or travel when the sun rose was necessary for the day's activities. The roads, the vehicles, and the buildings did not allow for the pace that modern life allows. One of my favorite films, A Christmas Carol, clearly shows the slower pace, even in the nineteenth century.

Another proverb that expresses advantages for rising early is, *Early to bed and early to rise, makes a man healthy, wealthy, and wise.* This proverb was printed as early as 1496, when it appeared in The Treatise of Fishing, and in 1639 by John Clarke. Americans became familiar with the proverb when Benjamin Franklin published it in 1735 in his Poor Richard's Almanac. It expresses the need for rest before one can expect to have health, wealth, and wisdom. (An opposite opinion on this proverb was published in The New Yorker in 1939 by James Thurber, *Early to bed and early to rise makes a male healthy and wealthy and **dead**.*)

Viewing sleep from another angle, the book of Proverbs in the Bible cautions about getting too much sleep. "How long wilt thou sleep, O sluggard? When wilt thou arise out of thy sleep? Yet a little sleep, a little slumber, a little folding of the hands to sleep. So shall thy poverty come as one that travelleth, and thy want as an armed man. " Proverbs 6: 9 – 11. Too much sleep will bring the opposite results. Early risers will avoid sleeping late.

Sleep is necessary for everyone, and sufficient sleep is necessary for one to perform their best work. Benjamin Franklin's proverb does not guarantee the results mentioned, but no proverb is a guarantee. It is a general truth or bit of advice. Unless circumstances dictate otherwise, it would probably be wise to follow the proverb.

ELECTRICITY CONTROLS OUR LIVES

Our bodies have electricity. We are electrical beings. Electricity controls our lives. Generally, atoms have no charge, with the atoms having the same number of protons and electrons. An atom has a positive charge when it loses an electron and a negative charge when it gains an electron. As these negatively charged electrons move through our bodies, we produce electricity. Without electricity, our brains would not function. They could not tell our mouths to eat, our hands to write, or our legs to walk because the brain must send electrical signals to our mouths, hands, and feet for them to operate. All activity in our bodies operates from the impulses sent by our brains.

Without electricity, there would be no functional infrastructure. Power plants and batteries produce the electricity needed to live our lives. The electricity sent through power lines runs our appliances (refrigerators, microwaves, dishwashers, etc.), televisions, vacuum cleaners, lights, and computers. It allows us to enjoy heat in the winter from furnaces and cool air in the summer from air conditioning units. Any equipment or machinery plugged into a wall requires electricity for it to function. Without electricity, we would be using coal and candles again.

Businesses are very dependent on their power. They need it to power their lights, computers, printers, copiers, fax machines, etc. Only the lighting would be possible without electricity. (Coal and candles.). Security would be lock and key or bolt. Employees or guests could no longer card in; they would be issued keys to access their business or hotel room. Banks could no longer wire funds. Without elevators, tall buildings would no longer be feasible. The infrastructure across the country would be irrelevant without the power to deliver to those who need it.

Batteries are used instead of electrical wires in many instances. Flashlights, cell phones, laptop computers, and vehicles are dependent on batteries. Cellphones and laptop computers require a power source for recharging. Cars, trucks, motorcycles, heavy machinery, etc. , need batteries to power their headlights, interior lights, power seats, and equipment. Alternators can produce the electrical energy needed to recharge the batteries in vehicles.

What does it feel like to be dependent on electricity? You may consider yourself to be independent, but unless you are living off the grid and traveling by an animal (horse, ox, camel), you are dependent. Our modern society is so immersed in electricity, making our lives much easier (and much more complicated), that it feels impossible to return to the early 19th century. And who would want to return? Our opportunities to travel, to invent or innovate, and to enjoy life are greater and more exciting than they have ever been.

Though I'm dependent on the grid, I like to enjoy some independence. I don't know enough about bitcoin or quantum mechanics (And you might say electricity) to comfortably comment on them. From what I do know about them, I don't care for either to make a change in my lifestyle. My main concern is AI. It's confusing to know what is true and what is false on YouTube. It seems a lot of material is either for PR or propaganda. Fortunately, there are lots of choices for news and information, and they can be turned off with the flip of an electrical switch or the touch of a screen.

COMFORT ZONES

We all have our comfort zones: places or situations where we feel comfortable. Homes, the neighborhood, schools, churches, restaurants, businesses, malls, the mountains, and the beach can be places of comfort. They become familiar to us over time, so we are at ease there. Being with family, schoolmates, coworkers, and neighbors allows us to be ourselves and to feel comfortable. We establish comfort zones at these places and with these people.

Let's consider the comfort zone of home. As we grow up, our strongest relationships should be with our families. We develop bonds with our parents and siblings. The basic needs for food, clothing, and shelter are provided by our parents. We depend on them to fulfill these responsibilities, and as they do, we become comfortable in the family. The sibling rivalry that occurs with brothers and sisters may be uncomfortable sometimes, but it is still part of our comfort zone.

The neighborhood is a place where relationships are developed in our childhood with boys and girls as we age. Each other's likes and dislikes are learned. Interactions are made where playing, partying, and participating in sports can be enjoyed. Engaging in these activities helps prepare children for learning as they begin school. The neighborhood comfort zone can be extended to school, as they attend school with some of the neighborhood kids. Comfort zones are disrupted when the family moves, and new relationships and new comfort zones must be built.

My favorite comfort zone is church. Outside of my family, my best friends are from church. Our Sunday School offers a host of activities where relationships can be built. Annual retreats, alternating between the beach and the mountains, monthly luncheons for the class, Spring and Fall dinners in members' homes, and monthly newsletters offer opportunities for members to expand their comfort zone in the class. One can sense that people are in their comfort zone from the fellowship expressed in the activities.

Eating out is certainly an enjoyable activity, so people have comfort zones in restaurants where the food tastes good. Those who enjoy steak may have a favorite steak place; those who prefer seafood may have a seafood restaurant; those who relish hamburgers may have a favorite hamburger joint as their comfort zone. To each his own, and everyone must eat, so having a comfort zone eating out can be an enjoyable experience. (You should have your home as a comfort zone, but who wants to eat at home all the time? Get out and enjoy a comfort zone with friends!)

PICNICS

Summertime is finally here! Vacations, traveling, time off to do your own thing. It's time to enjoy life with the decisions you make for yourself and your family as you get away from the mundane day-to-day existence. There are so many choices that you can make. The beach, the mountains, the lake, and theme parks are a few possibilities. You can plan for a week or for a few days away. Or you can plan for a staycation, staying close to home and avoiding the overnight expenses of vacations. One choice for a staycation is to picnic in a park, in the mountains, or by a lake or river.

Picnics offer a wonderful opportunity to get away. Just the two of you, you and your friends, your family, or a church group may enjoy the time together as you chat and chomp at a picnic. Planning, of course, is necessary to enjoy a good picnic. The venue and time must be determined. If a reservation is required, that should be made ahead of time. If the picnic will occur outdoors, the weather forecast must be considered. There should be a consensus on the food that will be eaten. If food will be cooked at the picnic (hot dogs, hamburgers), then a good ice chest is needed to hold the ice that will keep the food fresh.

After the planning has been made, the food has been packed, and the car is prepared for the trip, it's time to travel. Do you enjoy traveling? It can be fun traveling to your destination as you look forward to your picnic. If just you and your wife or husband have a picnic, conversations about past enjoyable experiences can be shared. I enjoy reminiscing and imagine a couple would enjoy it, too. If the family is traveling together, the kids can play 'I Spy' or word games to pass the time. Strengthening relationships along the way can set the mood for a pleasant picnic.

After arriving at the destination, it's time to set up. A tablecloth should be placed on the picnic table, with the ice chest and any bags placed on top. The food can be cooked while the kids explore. Places can be made for each person at the table. Plates, utensils, napkins, and drinks are placed for each person. When the kids return from exploring, it's time to eat.

Some things cannot be controlled at picnics, especially when they are held outside. Weather is one of those events, but with proper planning, the forecast will be known beforehand, so precautions will be taken. Mosquitoes, ants, and wild animals may be uninvited guests who want to join the picnic. They can be discouraged with swatting, sprays, or shouts, but it may be best to just endure them. They add to your experience and can be conversion pieces in later dialogues with friends. Many of the unexpected activities should not prevent you from having a good time with a picnic.

WILLPOWER

Willpower is an attribute that everyone has, though some exercise their willpower more than others. While willpower itself is not good or evil, it can manifest itself for good or evil purposes. People inherit inclinations to behave in certain manners, and their behaviors help develop their personalities. Of the four personality types (A, B, C, and D), people with Type A personalities tend to have stronger wills as they strive to achieve.

When personalities clash, the one with the stronger will tends to prevail. Simple decisions, such as 'where to go out for dinner,' can be decided by majority vote. If the strong-willed person decides on a different restaurant, that decision may prevail. Decisions made by majority vote can be overridden by a strong will. Willpower should be exercised carefully, especially with family and friends.

Strong-willed people often win playing sports, at least in their younger years. As they move up the sports ladder, they meet more athletes with strong wills. If the sport is tennis, track, or some sport where they compete individually, the one with the stronger will may win, assuming that they are athletically equal. In team sports, a collective will is needed to compete for the win. Strong wills can be defeated by fatigue or illness, but they are assets in competition.

Fathers and mothers with strong wills must be careful around each other and especially around their children. An unkind word with good intentions is still an unkind word and may have lasting consequences. It may break the spirit instead of the will and confuse the child about the intended purpose of the word. If the child has earned a stronger punishment (a spanking?), caution must be taken with the administration of it. Anger combined with a strong will can be devastating. Not only the child but the parent may be punished for correcting the child by going overboard with the correction.

Not everyone has a strong will. (Thank goodness!). A lot of decisions are made by consensus, where people with strong and weak wills can contribute. These decisions may decide what to eat, where to go on vacation, and when to go to bed. Unimportant decisions should be made without argument, but important decisions may require some discussion. If a consensus is not reached after discussion, someone must make the final decision. That person may have more experience or more understanding of what is needed. It may or may not be an individual with a strong will.

ENJOYING LIFE

Life was given to be enjoyed. With eyes to see, ears to hear, noses to smell, taste buds to taste, and nerves to feel, our bodies were created to enjoy the universe around us. We use our eyes to read, to drive, and to view the scenery when we travel. (Have you seen the sun rise or set over the ocean? It's an amazing sight.) We need our eyes to cook meals, to write letters, to take tests, to see colors and movement, and to fully appreciate the beauty of nature.

With our ears, we can hear the sounds around us. Nature provides a symphony of sounds where birds are singing, crickets are chirping, frogs are croaking, dogs are barking, and cats are meowing. We can hear the lawnmower mowing, the traffic moving, and planes flying. Our ears can listen to good music from the early 1900s until now. (Just ask Alexa. "Alexa, play songs from 1914 or 1920 or 1930. " Mention a year and she will play songs from that year.) Communication is made with our mouths as we hear one another talk. Seeing and hearing are probably the two senses that we treasure the most as we use them to express ourselves to the world and develop relationships in the world.

If you are like me, you enjoy the taste of good food. Our taste buds distinguish sweet from not sweet, hot from cold, bland from spicy, and salty from non-salty. Foods may be flavored according to taste. Some people enjoy their food warm, maybe even hot, while others are satisfied with room temperature. Some like spicy foods while some like bland foods better. While taste may not be a vital sense, it can certainly make eating a lot more enjoyable.

Smell can be a wonderful sense to appreciate when it is time to eat. A juicy steak cooking on the grill can enhance the appetite of the one waiting to eat it as he savors the fragrant smell of the steak cooking.

Smelling can also help discover when a food is not good to eat. Rotten or poisonous food might be detected by the smell, so smelling can help keep someone from getting sick or worse. Flowers release aromatic scents that our noses detect for us to smell. Men buy flowers on Valentine's Day or Mother's Day so their sweeties or mothers can enjoy the fragrances. People enjoy the spring when flowers begin to blossom and their perfumes fill the air.

Our bodies hold our eyes, our ears, our noses, our taste buds, and our nerves through which we make ourselves known to the world. Our nerves provide the impulses that make our other senses functional. Without nerves, the other senses would be useless. Our bodies express our emotions of happiness, sadness, love, hate, trust, fear, and surprise. We touch and feel a baby's soft skin, a lover's tender kiss, and a friend's hug. As we grow, we become more coordinated. From turning over, to standing, to walking, to running, our bodies grow more accustomed to living on earth. The more coordinated we are, the better we can enjoy activities and the more we can compete.

Value life. Value all the tools that you have for enjoying life. Take care of your eyes, your ears, and your nose. Be careful about what you eat and drink, and please take care of your body. It's the only body that you will have in this life, and it is frightfully short. Believe me, I'm a septuagenarian.

GRAVEYARDS

Graveyards can be very spooky, especially after dark. There's some uneasiness walking through a graveyard, thinking about those once alive, now dead and buried. You may sense that uneasiness reading Dracula or viewing a horror movie where a graveyard is included in the plot. The following dialogue expresses the feelings one might have.

Two boys in a graveyard, out of sight, were dividing up pecans under an old pecan tree. 'One for me, one for you, one for me, one for you. ' As they divided up the pecans, several dropped down toward the road. A boy passing by on a bicycle heard them. Though he couldn't see them, he could hear, 'One for me, one for you, one for me, one for you. ' Thinking he knew what was happening, he hurried toward town, where he met an old man, hobbling along with a cane.

'Mister, the Lord and Satan are in the graveyard dividing up the souls. '

'Boy, you don't know what you're talking about. '

'No, it's true. You can hear them talking. '

The old man was curious and hobbled with the boy toward the graveyard. As they approached the graveyard, they heard the boys. The old man suggested that they should try to see the Lord. As they peered through the darkness, trying to see, they heard the boys, 'One for me, one for you, one for me, one for you. That's all. Now let's get those nuts down by the road and we'll be done. ' They say the old man beat the boy back to town.

Our senses seem to become more alert at graveyards, especially old ones where graves have been there for generations. Our imaginations soar, influenced by books, movies, and the trepidation of the unknown.

You may remember the story of Ichabod Crane in the Legend of Sleepy Hollow. His superstitions led him to make unreasonable decisions, leading to an uncertain fate. His story may reflect what we would feel in a cemetery if we let our imaginations get the best of us.

The words graveyards and cemeteries are similar in meaning. A graveyard is an older term, referring to burials next to a church. (Maybe church folk were thinking of the rapture and wanted the dead to rise with them when the Lord returned.) As populations increased, people were buried in plots away from the church. The land where people were buried away from churches was called a cemetery.

I suppose the feelings are no different whether you visit a graveyard or a cemetery. If you've read enough tall tales or heard enough scary stories of spirits haunting houses or graveyards, you may feel fear to visit one by yourself. Being confident in your understanding of the spirit world, little though it may be, can keep superstitions from invading your mind. You can have confidence in comforting those who've lost loved ones. Funerals will be opportunities to sympathize with the bereaved, and the burials can be times of joy when you know the deceased is in heaven.

BILLBOARD NUMBER ONE SONGS

Billboard began its list of best-selling songs, called the HOT 100, in 1958. Since I was a teenager through most of the 1960s and enjoyed music, many of the earlier songs are familiar. I hope the following list of top songs from 1958 through 2000 triggers some nostalgia in you, as it has done in me.

1958 – Poor Little Fool by Ricky Nelson

1959 – Venus by Frankie Avalon

1960 – Theme from A Summer Place by Percy Faith

1961 – Travelin' Man by Ricky Nelson

1962 – The Loco-Motion by Little Eva

1963 – Surfin' U. S. A. by the Beach Boys

1964 – I Want to Hold Your Hand by The Beatles

1965 – Wooly Bully by Sam the Sham & the Pharaohs

1966 – California Dreamin' by The Mamas & the Papas

1967 – To Sir with Love by Lulu

1968 – Hey Jude by The Beatles

1969 – Sugar, Sugar by The Archies

1970 – Bridge Over Troubled Waters Simon and Garfunkel

1971 – Joy to the World by Three Dog Night

1972 – The First Time Ever I Saw Your Face by Roberta Flack

1973 – Tie a Yellow Ribbon Round the Ole Oak Tree by Tony Orlando and Dawn

1974 – The Way We Were by Barbara Streisand

1975 – Love Will Keep Us Together by Captain & Tennille

1976 – Silly Love Songs by Wings

1977 – Tonight's the Night (Gonna Be Alright) by Rod Stewart

1978 – Shadow Dancing by Andy Gibb

1979 – My Sharona by The Knack

1980 – Call Me by Blondie

1981 – Bette Davis Eyes by Kim Carnes

1982 – Physical by Olivia Newton-John

1983 – Every Breath You Take by The Police

1984 – When Doves Cry by Prince

1985 – Careless Whisper by Wham!

1986 - That's What Friends Are for by Dionne Warwick

1987 – Walk Like an Egyptian by The Bangles

1988 – Faith by George Michael

1989 – Look Away by Chicago

1990 – Hold On by Wilson Phillips

1991 – (Everything I Do) I Do It for You by Bryan Adams

1992 – End of the Road by Boyz II Men

1993 – I Will Always Love You by Whitney Houston

1994 – The Sign by Ace of Base

1995 – Gangsta's Paradise by Coolio

1996 – Macarena (Bayside Boys Mix) by Los Del Rio

1997 – Candle in the Wind 1997/Something about the Way You Look Tonight by Elton John

1998 – Too Close by Next

1999 – Believe by Cher

2000 – Breathe by Faith Hill

RELIGION

Is religion important? Is it necessary for people to have religion? What does the word religion mean? The word must be understood before one can know if he or she is religious. One definition of religion is: a set of beliefs concerning the cause, nature, and purpose of the universe. Another is: the life or state of a monk, nun, etc. A third definition states that religion is something a person believes in and follows devotedly. It is this third definition that we will consider.

A person may be a Roman Catholic, a Protestant, a Jehovah's Witness, a Seventh Day Adventist, a Moslem, or a Hindu and be considered to have religion. But is that person religious? Does belonging to an organization with a set of beliefs make one a religious person? Does following the beliefs of the organization make one religious? Is simply having faith sufficient for one to be religious? The book of James in the New Testament says that faith without works is dead.

Two things are apparent in our definition of religion: having a belief in something and acting on that belief. A Roman Catholic may believe that he can pray to the Virgin Mary and use a rosary to count his prayers. A Moslem may practice his belief by bowing and praying five times a day toward Mecca. A Seventh Day Adventist may believe the Sabbath must be kept on Saturday, so he attends church on Saturday. These people are being religious by following the beliefs of their religion. They believe in God (or a god) and practice their religion to show their faith, to get closer to God, to soothe their conscience, or for some other reason, hoping that their efforts or works will gain them favor with God.

I stated earlier a reference from the book of James that "faith without works is dead. " Earlier in the same book, James gives his definition for religion: "Pure religion and undefiled before God and the Father is this, to visit the fatherless and widows in their affliction and to keep himself unspotted from the world. " He also said, "But be ye doers of the word, and not hearers only, deceiving your own selves. "

I believe working out your religion in everyday life is necessary to show your faith. Religion does not save your soul, but may act as a testimony and be evidence of the faith that you claim to have. It is important to have religion since we have spirits as well as bodies. Visiting the fatherless and widows and keeping yourself unspotted from the world may be evidence that you have the right spirit within you.

FUN WITH WORDS

You have heard the expression, "Sticks and stones may break my bones, but words can never hurt me. " I don't know where that saying originated, but we know that it is not true. Words can and do hurt – but not now because we're going to have fun with words.

Let's start with a movie, Mary Poppins, starring Julie Andrews and Dick Van Dyke. Do you recall the word made famous in that movie? It's a super long word – 34 letters long. The word is Supercalifragilisticexpialidocious, and it is one of the songs in the movie. According to this Walt Disney film from 1964, the word means, 'something to say when you have nothing to say. ' (I've heard people say all kinds of things when they have nothing to say.). The word was even used on Wheel of Fortune in 1997 under the category "Really Long Title. "

One aspect of words is ambiguity. That is, two words may sound the same but have different meanings. Suppose I asked you for the definition of tents. Would your answer be, "Tents is the plural of tent, which means a portable shelter of canvas supported by poles or a metal frame. " That is a definition for tents. Would a definition of tense be, "showing mental or emotional strain? " Yes, that is also a valid definition.

Consider the following dialogue: A man named Mr. Jones goes to a psychiatrist. "Doc, you've got to help me. I have a problem sleeping because I keep having weird dreams. Sometimes I see myself as a wigwam and other times as a teepee. "

"Ok, Mr. Jones, let me be sure that I understand your problem. You are disturbed by dreams where you see yourself as a wigwam or a teepee. Is that correct? "

"That's right, Doc. Sometimes I'm a wigwam, sometimes I'm a teepee. Can you help me, Doc? "

Yes, Mr. Jones, I think I have the answer to your problem. You're two tense (two tents).

Is he right? Is he saying tense or tents? Yes. Both. Fun With Words.

Ok, that's enough with jokes. Let's look at another word – sucker. You will recall the expression, "There's a sucker born every minute. " It is attributed to P. T. Barnum. What kind of sucker is mentioned in that expression? Is it a lollipop? Could it be a thick-lipped North American freshwater fish? Would you call that sucker a shoot from a subterranean stem or root? Each of these, lollipop, fish, and shoot, is a definition of a sucker. None of them is the meaning expressed in Mr. Barnum's sentence. P. T. Barnum's sucker was a person who was easily cheated. I suppose he thought that the world was full of gullible people.

Suppose you heard that a Good Samaritan provided succor to a man whom he rescued from a burning building. You know that succor here is not the same sucker linked to Mr. Barnum. They sound the same but have entirely different meanings. Succor means "timely aid in distress. " When you hear words that sound like other words, you must use discretion to determine the correct meaning.

MOTTOS OF COUNTRIES

Philippines – For God, People, Nature, and Country

Aruba – One Happy Island

Spain – Further Beyond

Tanzania – Freedom and Unity

Trinidad & Tobago – Together we aspire, together we achieve

Uruguay – Liberty or Death

Luxembourg – We wish to remain what we are

Japan - Endless discovery

Brazil – Order and Progress

Venezuela – God and Federation

France – Livery, Equality, Fraternity

Germany - Unity, Justice and Freedom

India – Truth Alone Triumphs

Chile – By Reason or by Force

Argentina – In unity and freedom

Canada – From Sea to Sea

Peru – Firm and Happy for the Union

Egypt – Freedom, Socialism, and Unity

Morocco – God, Homeland, King

Turkey – Peace at Home, Peace in the World

Lebanon – All of us, for our country

Iraq – God is the Greatest

Iran – Independence, Freedom, the Islamic Republic

Uzbekistan – Power is in Justice

Belize – Under the Shade I Flourish

EL Salvador – God, Union, Liberty

Honduras – Free, Sovereign, and Independent

Nicaragua – In God We Trust

Bolivia – Unity is Strength

Paraguay – Peace and Justice

Uruguay – Freedom or Death

Pakistan – Faith, Unity, Discipline

Afghanistan – There is no God but Allah, Muhammad is the messenger of God

Suriname – Justice – Piety – Trust

Indonesia – Unity in Diversity

South Africa – Diverse People Unite

CROWDS

Crowds. You can't escape them, especially in a big city where I live. People are in the grocery stores, in the malls, at concerts, on vacations, and on the freeways (vehicles). All kinds of people populate crowds; tall people, short people, fat people, slim people, light-skinned people, dark-skinned people, men, women, boys, and girls. (On the freeways, you might see trucks, trailers, cars, vans, and motorcycles.)

I tend to like crowds because I like people. There are exceptions, of course, such as when I'm in a hurry. Thoughts go through my mind in the grocery store or in the mall when people pass by. Does that tall, young man play basketball? How much does that man weigh? Are all those children hers? Wow! That lady is a knockout!

What is it about crowds that people don't like? Are they afraid of closed spaces, and does it cause them claustrophobia? Are they afraid that someone might steal from them? Perhaps they are in a hurry, and a crowd would slow them down. A wreck on the interstate could certainly slow down the traffic. Rubberneckers keep traffic backed up even after the wreck has been cleared from the highway.

What can be done to assuage emotions caused by the crowds? Patience is required when people are delayed by crowds. On the highway, unless you know the roads where you can detour around a wreck, it would be best to wait it out. In a grocery store, you might look for the shortest line or the line that moves quickly. Or you might ring up the groceries in a self-checkout line. Going shopping when the store is not crowded is another option.

The malls may not have crowds except at certain times of the day or year. Days close to holidays such as Valentine's Day, Mother's Day, Father's Day, Halloween, Thanksgiving, and Christmas can be crowded as people shop for presents, candy, or food for special meals. People travel mostly on holidays, so highways and airports can be especially crowded as people visit family and friends.

It is virtually impossible to avoid crowds at popular sporting events or concerts. Going early to get your seat can help avoid some of the crowd. When you really enjoy the events, the crowd should not be too disturbing. You may enjoy the occasion even more if you can enjoy the crowd. Be like me and enjoy watching individuals at the events. Some of the thoughts that run through my mind may run through your mind. Does she think she looks good in that outfit? Is that child lost? Where did he find that girl?

I've looked at crowds from both sides now. They can be fun, and they can be frustrating. How do you see clouds?

NUTRITION

Ok. Everyone who wants to be sick, raise your hand. Just as I thought, no hands are raised. Of course, no one wants to be sick. Everyone in their right mind wants to be healthy. Good health requires good nutrition. My journey toward good nutrition began in 1977. Friends invited me to a meeting where I learned about food supplements; plant-based products providing protein, vitamins, minerals, and more. The information that I learned helped me begin taking products that I continue to this day.

Three products were particularly important in beginning a nutrition program: protein, multivitamins, and herbs. The herbs were designed to clean the colon and glands, but especially the colon. With a clean colon, nutrients can be absorbed more readily into the body. Thus, nutrition must begin with a colon cleansing, removing the excess food and waste. Once the colon is cleansed, the protein supplement can be taken to help build the cells. Then, the multivitamin with vitamins and minerals should be swallowed to help with metabolism. Each of these supplements, protein, multivitamins, and herbs, should be taken with food, which is why they are called food supplements. They supplement your meals, providing any nutrition that is missing in your regular diet.

Through the years, I have continued to take these products and have added more to them. Though the multivitamin has these vitamins, I have added Vitamin C, Vitamin E, and B-Complex, lecithin, and alfalfa products to the program. A calcium supplement and a vitamin D supplement are available, but I'm satisfied that sufficient calcium and vitamin D are in the multivitamin. Plus, I get vitamin D from the sun. The protein supplement is soybean-based, so all the essential amino acids, amino acids that your body cannot produce, are available. The protein is offered in vanilla and cocoa powder, but my choice is vanilla.

Unless you grow your own food (animals and plants) or get it from a source that does, it is vital to supplement your diet. (Even growing your own food requires diligence to ensure that the food is nutritious.) Much of store-bought food is highly processed, causing loss of or deterioration in the food's value. Supplementation helps provide the nutrition that was lost in the processing.

Have you heard of the carnivore diet? This diet allows you to eat meats (beef, pork, chicken, turkey, etc.), fish, and eggs, but no fruits or vegetables. It sounds delicious; juicy T-bone steaks, broiled flounder, scrambled eggs, until you realize that it is. No tomatoes, no potatoes, no green vegetables are allowed. Also, desserts, cookies, cake, and ice cream are not part of this diet. The carnivore diet requires a lot of discipline. One must decide whether the health benefits gained would be worth the sacrifice made.

The carnivore diet does sound better to me than a vegan diet. I certainly enjoy eating meat, fish, and eggs, and eliminating them would be a sacrifice for me. However, I enjoy eating nuts, seeds, fruits, and vegetables, so I'll continue eating food that I like and supplementing my food with food supplements.

THE BEACH

Ah, the beach! Fun times are here again! Who doesn't enjoy spending time at the seashore? Many people enjoy it so much that they move there or buy some property there. It takes several hours to visit the beach from where I live, but that doesn't stop me from enjoying it several times a year. As a grandpa, there is more to enjoy than when I was single. As the family grows, so do the opportunities to have fun. I have found that the grandchildren like the ocean even more than grandpa.

Sand: Getting sand on your shoes at the beach is a given. Whether you go barefoot or wear flip-flops, sandals, slides, or shoes on the shore, you will find that the sand will cling to you. A faucet or shower is necessary to remove the sand before you return to your vehicle or room. Of course, getting to the shore on bare feet can be a problem when the sand is hot. If you don't run, you could get second or third-degree burns on your feet. (I have a friend with diabetes who didn't feel the heat as he walked, so his feet got burned.)

The beach is also a good place to search for wedding rings, engagement rings, coins, and tackle lost in the sand. I bought a cheap metal detector and found a 4-ounce lead fishing weight. Another search can be made for seashells. Most seashells that you find will be broken, so it may take time to find complete shells. Perhaps the best time to search is early morning, especially after a storm. Types of shells that are not normally found may appear after a storm washes them up on shore.

Besides seashells, sharks' teeth can be found on or under the sand. The best place I've found for sharks' teeth is Holden Beach in southeastern North Carolina. Sifting through the sand at low tide or digging through the sand when it is wet may yield good results. You may have difficulty finding complete teeth, but keep looking because they are there. If you are fortunate, you may find a very large tooth of a Megalodon shark. The largest Megalodon tooth found was over seven inches long! (If you don't want to search for sharks' teeth, you could buy them at one of the many beach stores that sell them.)

I love riding the waves in the ocean. (Yes, even Grandpa rides waves.) Riding the waves before they crash is easier than after they crash. You must use judgement to determine when to ride the waves. Just plant your feet and push hard enough so your head will be above the wave. Or you can let the wave pass over you and push through it. With the right timing, you will come flying out on the other side! I have bodysurfed, but that is too tough for Grandpa now. (I'll leave surfing, by board or body, to the younger generation.)

A final comment for the beach concerns places to eat. Seafood lovers know that the beach is a good place for great seafood. Not only is the food good, but the location may enhance the experience. (Unlike the food on the moon, great food, no atmosphere. Sorry, I had to say that.) My favorite place for seafood is Calabash, North Carolina, where several good seafood restaurants are located. Captain John's, Captain Nance's, and Dockside are a few. I ate at Ella's a few times before it burned to the ground. When it reopens, I plan to return.

I hope you do or will enjoy the beach as much as I do. It is a wonderful place to enjoy with family or friends – or even by yourself.

PICTURES

There are a lot of synonyms for pictures; copies, depictions, descriptions, drawings, duplicates, engravings, film, illustrations, likenesses, lookalikes, replicas, and similitudes to name a few. We view pictures in motion on film, on television, and on the internet, and we see still pictures in drawings, engravings, and illustrations. With our cellphones, we snap shots of families, friends, nature, and more. Our cellphone 'libraries' hold thousands of shots we have snapped over the years.

Artists fill museums, businesses, and homes with illustrations of weather, weddings, and wildlife, while photographers take real-life pictures of the same. When you are on vacation, you may notice the pictures on the walls of the hotel room where you sleep and on the restaurant walls where you dine. It would be surprising to see bare walls in either your hotel room or in the restaurant. Pictures are ubiquitous.

You may also notice pictures in your mail or email. Ads promoting vacation destinations showcase the amenities that they offer. They may depict the comforts of the hotel or resort room, the inviting outdoor pool, or the delicious continental breakfast. (Not all continental breakfasts are delicious.). You may see the nearby ocean or theme park as an attraction. The pictures provided appeal to the person's desire to travel, to be with friends, and to enjoy new experiences. Of course, the ads accentuate the positive and avoid any negatives, but what else would you expect?

Other places where pictures are presented are magazines. Many magazines are filled with pictures. Sports Illustrated holds depictions of athletes and athletic events; National Geographic carries pictures of cultures captured from around the world; Travel and Leisure highlights vacation destinations appealing to travelers. You can enjoy the pictures as you read about sports, learn about life around the world, and anticipate traveling to far-away places for a vacation.

There is an aspect of pictures where discretion is needed. Parents, babysitters, and guardians must be careful about what they allow children to see. Television not only shows pictures, but the pictures are moving! The excitement created by a picture is enhanced by its rhythm, its movement. A child would be much more influenced to do something, either good or bad, by seeing action rather than just looking at a still picture. The responsibility to limit his/her exposure to television must be taken seriously.

That brings us to the internet. The whole world of ideas, conversations, and pictures is available to the viewer of the internet. If one can be addicted to what they see, the internet can lead to that addiction. If children are to avoid this addiction, their exposure to what they see must be carefully guarded. Since they cannot always be so carefully protected, the parents should notice any changes in their behavior that may suggest an addiction. They must develop a good rapport with their children, so their children will have the confidence to confide in their parents.

Pictures show life and can reveal expressions of joy or sorrow, hope or despair, peace or distress. They can encourage or discourage. Our fast-paced society paints pictures everywhere, but not all pictures should be viewed by everyone. We must use discretion for ourselves, our families, and everyone that we influence when we look at pictures, whether in print, on television, or on the internet. Meanwhile, enjoy the pictures you see in magazines, in books, and in shots captured on your cellphones.

SEARCHING FOR COINS

Do you take daily walks? If so, what do you have for an Incentive? Are the expected health benefits, the hope of a longer life, or maybe a better retirement, an incentive for you? Perhaps the sheer joy of walking is enough to stimulate you to walk.

My incentive to walk is the expectation of finding coins. Lifting weights and doing isometric exercises are exercises that I do inside. The incentive for these exercises is to stay healthy and have the energy to work around the house. Mowing the grass is much easier after a round of exercises. When I walk, though, I hope to find some coins.

Have you ever searched for coins day after day? I find that it can be rewarding (in a small way) and frustrating. It is exciting to find coins of different values. Let me share some of my experiences searching for coins.

Almost all the coins that I find are pennies, nickels, dimes, and quarters, though a 5-peso piece from the Dominican Republic, a Sacagawea dollar, and a two-dollar Canadian coin were also found. It would be a big surprise for me to find a half-dollar coin or a silver dollar coin, or a coin worth a lot of money. The highest value of coins found in one day was $2. 20, so my search for coins is not a second job.

Two phrases that I use in my search are baseball terms: grand slam and hitting for the cycle. A grand slam in baseball is when the batter hits a home run with the bases loaded, so four runs cross the plate. Hitting for the cycle means one person hits a single, a double, a triple, and a home run in the same game. In searching for coins, both terms refer to finding a penny, a nickel, a dime, and a quarter on the same day. It's been done several times, and twice on two separate days.

Coins are found in many places where people drop them. I have found them on my street, at convenience stores, at gas stations, at a vehicle service shop, at car washes, and in apartment parking lots. There are many new apartment complexes close to where I live, so most of my searches are done there. Most of the coins are found there.

If you have searched for coins, you probably know that what appears to be a coin from a distance is not. Do you recall seeing small, round, white circles? You might think it is a dime until you get up close. Then you realize it's not even a coin. It falls from the sky. I've had to look closely to see that it is from a bird and not from the mint. Other dime lookalikes are circular batteries. You may see a flash of silver on the ground or pavement. As you get closer, you notice that it is round, silverish, and the size of a dime. As you reach down to pick the dime up, you realize that it is not a dime. If you have good eyesight, you may notice that it is smooth, so you don't pick it up. My eyesight is not too good, so I've picked up several batteries.

After finding the coins, I bring them home and deposit them into separate containers. The pennies go into a round ceramic container, the nickels are dropped into a glass jar, the dimes are put into a pink piggy bank, and the quarters are inserted into a ceramic football. When enough coins are collected, they are rolled and taken to the bank to be exchanged for bills. A full roll holds fifty pennies, or forty nickels, or fifty dimes, or forty quarters. Few if any of the coins are in mint condition, so I haven't spent much time searching for coins of value. Almost all the coins have wear, so they are worth only face value.

If you decide to search for coins, good luck. It is certainly not lucrative, and sometimes you may not find any. You may have to go past one hundred cars in the parking lot before finding even a penny. But be patient and remember that walking is more important than searching for coins. Diligently walking daily or several times a week will yield more benefits than finding dozens of coins.

EPITAPHS

Floyd Patterson – A Champion always

Joe DiMaggio – Grace, dignity, and elegance personified

Dean Martin – Everybody loves somebody sometime

Jayne Mansfield – We live to love you more each day

Gracie Allen and George Burns – Together again

Alexander the Great – A tomb now suffices him for whom the world was not enough

Edgar Allan Poe – Quoth the raven, "Nevermore"

Ritchie Valens – Come on let's go

Frank Sinatra – The best is yet to come

Mel Blanc – That's all folks

Spike Milligan – I told you I was ill

Billy Wilder – I'm a writer, but then nobody's perfect

Rodney Dangerfield – There goes the neighborhood

Merv Griffin – I will <u>not</u> be right back after this message

Jack Lemmon – JACK LEMMON in

Bette Davis – She did it the hard way

Robert Ford – The man who shot Jesse James

Rita Hayworth – To yesterday's companionship and tomorrow's reunion

Robert Lee Frost – I had a lover's quarrel with the world

Lucille Ball – You've Come Home

Jules Verne – Towards Immortality and Eternal Youth

Abraham Lincoln – Now he belongs to the ages

Ludolph van Ceulen-3.
14159265358979323846264338327950288

Joan Hackett – Go Away – I'm asleep

Dorothy Parker – Excuse my dust

John Belushi – I may be gone, but Rock and Roll lives on

Jackie Gleason – And away we go

Jack Dempsey – A Gentle Man and a gentleman

Lester Moore – Here lies Lester Moore. Four slugs from a 44, no Les, no more.

Hank Williams – I'll never get out of this world alive.

Johnny Cash – I Walk the Line

The following epitaphs are anonymous.

Here lies Johnny Yeast. Pardon me for not rising.

Here lies Ezekial Aikle, age 102. The good die young.

Here lies Ann Mann, who lived as an old maid but died an old Mann.

Here lies an atheist. All dressed up and no place to go.

She always said her feet were killing her, but nobody believed her.

FAMOUS LAST WORDS

Sometimes when a person dies, he says some last words to his nurse, his family, his friends, or whoever attends his bedside. His comments may express his faith, his failures. His need, his love, his hate, or a myriad of emotions. They may be a window to his soul. This chapter features actors, politicians, authors, sports figures, and more. (I cannot confirm that these are indeed their last words because I wasn't there.)In fact, I noticed that there are different versions of the last words for several of the people mentioned. (You might do your own research to see different last words for the same person.)

Anton Levey – Something is wrong; something is terribly wrong.

Bessie Smith – I'm going, but I'm going in the name of the Lord.

Frank Sinatra – I'm losing it.

Margaret Sander – A party. Let's have a party.

Herman Melville – God bless Captain Vere.

Bob Marley - Money can't buy life.

John Adams - Thomas Jefferson survives.

John Quincy Adams – This is the last of earth. I am content.

Marie Antoinette – Pardonnez-moi, monsieur.

Benjamin Franklin – A dying man can't do nothing easy.

Sir Arthur Conan Doyle – You are wonderful. (to his wife)

T. S. Eliot – Valerie (to his wife)

Groucho Marx – This is no way to live.

Pete Maravich – I feel great.

Vladimer Lenin – Good dog.

Sir Winston Churchill – I'm bored with it all.

Do Diddley – Wow.

Steve Jobs – Oh wow! Oh wow! Oh wow!

Truman Capote – Mama. Mama. Mama.

James Brown – I'm going away tonight.

General John Sedgwick – Oh God, I've been murdered

Robert E. Lee – Strike the tent.

Emily Dickinson – I must go, for the fog is rising.

Salvador Dali – I do not believe in my death.

Jack Daniel's – One last drink, please.

FDR – I have a terrific headache,

Voltaire – Now is not the time for making new enemies.

Judas Iscariot – I have sinned in that I have betrayed innocent blood.

Stephen – Lord, lay not this sin to their charge.

Michael Landon – You're right. It's time. I love you all.

Humphrey Bogart – Goodbye, kid. Hurry back.

Charles Gussman – And now for a final word from our sponsor.

Elvis Presley – I'm going to the bathroom to read.

Leonardo Da Vinci – I have offended God and mankind because my work did not reach the quality it should have.

Jackie Robinson – A Life is not important except in the impact it has on other lives.

Thomas Hobbs – I am about to take a leap into the dark.

Thomas Payne – If ever the Devil had an agent, I have been that one.

Sir Thomas Scott – I am doomed to perdition by the just judgment of the Almighty.

Sir Francis Newport – Oh, the insufferable pangs of Hell!

Charles IX – What shall I do? I am lost forever! Oh, I have done wrong.

David Strauss – My philosophy leaves me utterly forlorn!

D L Moody – God is calling me, and I must go.

Alexander the Great – To the strongest.

Ellen G White – I know in whom I have believed.

Timothy McVeigh – I am the master of my fate; I am the captain of my soul.

REVENGE

You know the feeling. Someone has stolen from you or embarrassed you, or hurt you in some way. They have done you wrong in such a manner that you want to repay them. You want to retaliate; you want revenge.

Revenge can take many forms since there are several ways that one may avenge oneself. It can be inflicted on the body or the property of the perpetrator. His livelihood or even his family may suffer from the avenger's wrath. The vengeance could be immediate, perhaps without clear thinking, or it may take time to develop a scheme to "get even".

Maybe the person wronged does not care to even the score, but wants to teach a lesson to the wrongdoer. He doesn't want his 'pound of flesh' but is interested in the welfare of the person who did him wrong. There is no desire to inflict the wrongdoer with punishment that will not benefit him. He wants the wrongdoer to learn that he has done wrong and that continuing that behavior will hurt him eventually.

Revenge should not be inflicted when one has been hurt or demoted, or robbed. It could lead to circuitous behavior. (You hit me, so I'll hit you. You demoted me, so I'm going to sabotage the production line.)These reactions do not alleviate the problem and tend to escalate it. Before taking any action against the wrongdoer, one should be patient and consider what should be done. Quick decisions often lead to bad consequences.

I think any vengeance taken should be taken by a higher authority. In a family, the matter must be brought to the parents. The teacher, principal, or headmaster should be involved in a school setting. Where the event happened in a business environment, the supervisor, manager, or the boss should be involved. If a crime has been committed, it becomes a legal matter for the police to decide on any punishment. In any event, the person wronged must be careful to contact the right authority.

If vengeance is taken, it may be delivered by God through his agent, whether it is a teacher, manager, principal, or police. Or God may work through circumstances to teach or punish the guilty party. In many situations where one has been wronged, it is best to just drop the matter. Just let the matter go to remove any anger or animosity and avoid any future episodes. In the cases where the matter is dropped, it is hoped that the wrongdoer will come to his senses and change his attitude and his behavior.

EXERCISE

One, two, three, four. Up, down, up, down. Stop, go, stop, go. Whew! Exercising is exhausting! Considering the benefits that can be received, temporary exhaustion is gladly acceptable. Teams exercise to prepare for their next game, runners exercise to prepare for their next race, and individuals exercise to stay in shape. Aerobics exercise, hiking, skipping rope, and swimming are only a few activities people engage in to reach their goals. One source states that the five big exercises are squat, deadlift, bench press, overhead press, and pull-ups.

Our bodies are amazing creations, but they don't last indefinitely. Care must be used to keep our bodies healthy, to prevent sickness and weakness when it is possible. Eating healthy foods, avoiding dangerous activities, developing a good reading habit, getting sufficient sleep, and disciplining the time we spend online are actions where care is needed. Along with these activities, we should develop exercise routines that are appropriate for ourselves.

Being a septuagenarian, I need exercises to help me enjoy each day. I'm not as disciplined about exercising as I should be since I don't do it consistently. It's when I don't do them that I realize how necessary they are. A leg sprain or pain in various parts of my body testifies to the exercise that was needed but not done. Not a lot of work is needed; I'm not preparing for a spot on the Olympic team. I'm just trying to stay in good shape. (Everyone is in shape, it's just that some shapes are not as pleasant to see as others.)Let me share some of the exercises that I do.

Small weights are used in some of my routines. I have two three-pound weights, two five-pound weights, and an eight-pound weight. The three-pound and five-pound weights are part of the on-the-couch lifting. Lying on the couch, I do curls and presses, with either two weights in one hand or one weight in each hand. Sometimes, either one or both arms are stretched out behind my head, then raised directly above my head with a weight in one hand or both hands, or two weights in one hand. (Maybe I'm a couch potato, but I consider myself a couch exerciser. At least that is how I justify it.)

While lifting the weights, I am also lifting my legs. With a knee in one hand and a weight in the other, I bend my knee back and forth while lifting the weight. Or the leg may be extended to go up and down while the weight is lifted. Sometimes the legs are spread apart and opened and closed as my arms use the weights. To help the time go by, I may listen to Alexa. ("Alexa, play music from 1960. Alexa, play songs from Skeeter Davis. Alexa, play songs from The Association. ") Music soothes the soul as exercise stimulates the body. I recommend listening to music as you exercise.

Lying on a mat on the floor, I floor press the eight-pound weight. (It must be a floor press because I don't have a bench.)The number of reps varies. There may be twenty-five, fifty, seventy-five, or one hundred. I think the most reps at one time were one hundred seventy-five. The number of sets of reps varies, also. It is normally less than ten. Another exercise is to raise the arms straight up, extend the weight parallel to the floor, then straight up again. Only a few of these are repeated.

Finally, I walk. When I walk by myself, I search for coins. (Among other things, I found a wallet and credit card, both of which I turned in.). Walking is the best overall exercise for me and a good exercise for everyone who can walk. I highly recommend it and suggest walking with a friend or friends. But whether lifting weights or walking, please exercise. It is needed and it can be very enjoyable, but it is not immediately, then later it is.

PREFERENCES VERSUS CONVICTIONS

Choices are made every day, and we must choose from among the choices that are available. In college, a student must decide which courses to take. Some courses are required for a major, but choices are made from the electives that are offered. When one decides to marry, a mate is chosen. (Of course, the mate must accept your choice.)After marriage, many choices are made with input from both spouses; do we have children, how many children do we want, how many boys and how many girls should we have? (Ok, some choices are beyond our control!)

Choosing means preferring one instead of another. For a vacation, the choice may be between national or international, the beach or the mountains, Disney World or Universal Studios (or maybe both!)These preferences are optional and may be decided by parents or by a consensus of the whole family. The beach may be chosen from nostalgia or a desire to play in the ocean. Disney World may be chosen because the kids want to see Mickey and Minnie. These choices are generally not life-changing and are preferences. Where strong emotions are involved, where the decision involves something that must be done or must not be done, the choice is more than a preference. It is a conviction.

A conviction is a firm belief. Someone with a firm conviction will not compromise and will not change his mind. He is adamant in his resolve. It may be a diet (Keto, Vegan, Atkins, or Carnivore) that will be followed until the goal is reached. A man who is a confirmed bachelor is convicted of not marrying. He plans to remain single for the rest of his life. (Just wait for the right woman, and that conviction is shown to be a preference.). A woman may choose a career instead of children, so she is committed to staying single. Conviction is when one sets his face like a flint, so that his decision will not change. Of course, changing circumstances may change convictions. Or what was thought to be true was found to be false, so convictions change based on new knowledge.

When I think of conviction, I think of conscience. With a clear conscience and a good understanding of right and wrong, the conscience is convicted when the wrong decision is made. A conviction to do right is replaced by guilt for doing wrong. In the Christian faith, the wrong behavior should be confessed (to God) so the guilty person can be forgiven. When forgiveness is received, the person can renew or change his convictions. Convictions should not be taken lightly. If you make convictions, be firm in following them.

Preferences are choices that people make each day. They can be changed with no guilt involved. The conscience should not be bothered by changing vacation plans, or changing the menu, or planning a different itinerary. Convictions are firm choices that should not be changed except for unusual circumstances. It is wise to know if your choices are based on preference or conviction and to act accordingly. You can be happier keeping your convictions, though you may change your preferences from time to time.

TWO OF A KIND

Have you thought about how necessary two is in society? Marriage begins with two: a husband and a wife. In politics, there are two main parties. In sports, two teams or two people compete against each other. There are also good versus evil and right versus wrong.

Society has many competing factions as one against one or two (or more) against two (or more). In the United States, the Republicans run against the Democrats for positions and power in government. (Other parties run, but either the Republicans or the Democrats have won all the Presidential races and most of the other races for decades.)In the world, some governments allow freedom to their people while other governments enslave them. The sports world has competitions to determine winners, so one side wins and the other side loses.

Religions or faiths have opposing views. A faith of absolute values places good versus evil and right versus wrong. In the Christian faith, there are two destinies: heaven or hell. The destinies are determined by the choice that is made. Believe that Jesus paid for your sins and trust him forever, and heaven is your destiny. Without Jesus, you have chosen to pay for your own sins, so the only choice left is hell.

There are positive and negative numbers, addition and subtraction, multiplication and division, pluses and minuses. There are the binary numbers, 0 and 1, even numbers and odd numbers, rational numbers and irrational numbers, and prime and composite numbers. (I'm not making this stuff up.)

I think the words for the number two are choice and win. You choose a mate. You win in sports. You choose in a political race and hope that your candidate wins. Choose an incompatible mate, and you've made a bad choice. Play a vastly superior opponent in tennis, and you can expect to lose. Of course, it is more important to choose a good mate than to play any opponent in sports. The partner should be yours "until death do you part". The ideal marriage will last a lifetime. A sport can be played against different opponents again and again. In our society today, many have considered marriage as a sport and have entertained several partners. Perhaps the animal kingdom could serve as an example of marriage for life. Lots of birds, including swans and bald eagles, tend to mate for life.

Consider your own body. Many parts of your body come in twos. You have two hands, two feet, two arms, two legs, two eyes, two ears, and two nostrils. Internally, there are two kidneys and two hemispheres of your brain. If a hand, foot, arm, leg, eye, or ear is lost, the other should allow you to function, though at a reduced capacity. People can and do donate one of their kidneys to someone who needs one. (You're out of luck if you lose half of your brain.)

Your body has a right side and a left side. That helps explain why you have two of a kind for several parts. You are bilateral, so you have a right hand and left hand, a right foot and a left foot, and so forth. Much of the animal kingdom is created with two eyes and two ears, along with other bilateral parts. Creation began with two (Adam and Eve), and society continues to use two through technology. One may be the loneliest number, but two is a vital number in our society.

PHRASES – IDIOMS

Barking up the Wrong Tree

Beating around the Bush

Breaking the Ice

Biting the bullet

Break a Leg

Costas an Arm and a Leg

By the Skin of Your Teeth

Crying Over Spilled Milk

A Blessing in Disguise

Cutting Corners

Hit the Sack

A dime a Dozen

A Penny for your Thoughts

Assing Insult to Injury

Better Late than Never

A Bad Apple

At the Drop of a Hat

Curiosity Killed the Cat

Going Back to the Drawing Board

A Picture is Worth a Thousand Words

Easier Said than Done

A Piece of Cake

Felling Under the Weather

Parked Like Sardines

Killing Two Birds with one Stone

Hitting the Books

That Rings a Bell

Cut to the Chase

Up in the Air

Breaking the Bank

Living Hand to Mouth

Rule of Thumb

Cool as a Cucumber

Spice Things Up

Couch Potato

Not my Cup of Tea

Spill the Beans

Lose Tough

Twist Someone's Arm

That's the Last Straw

Making a Long Story Short

Pull Yourself Together

Ruffle One's Feathers

You Can Say that Again

It's not Rocket Science

East Does it

No Pain, No Gain

Time Flies when You're having Fun

Your Guess is as Good as Mine

Bent out of Shape

Speak of the Devil

One a Wild Goose Chase

Ignorance is Bliss

It's Raining Cats and Dogs

A Taste of Their Medicine

Takes Two to Tango

That's the Last Straw

To Cut Corners

To Go Dutch

To Have Sticky Fingers

To Sit TIght

GUMBALLS

The scientific name for what I call gumball trees is Liquidambar. Other names for this tree are hazel pine, bilsted, redgum, alligatorwood, and sweetgum. These trees grow round spiky objects called gumballs that look like the pictures you've seen of the COVID virus, round with pointed pieces sticking up uniformly from the gumball. They can't be eaten, they are no good for fertilizer (as far as I know), and they are a pain to remove from one's yard. The pain is that they drop from the trees for months.

I remove them by raking them. After raking them from the driveway and yard, I bag them as yard waste and take the bags to the curb. For two or three months, they are raked with the leaves, but after the leaves are gone, the gumballs keep coming down for months. All the gumballs need to be raked because stepping on them can cause s sprained ankle. Walking barefoot in the yard would certainly be a problem in the summertime. Any gumball stragglers hidden in the grass would be very uncomfortable to someone who stepped on one.

Removing the prickly gumballs can be frustrating when a strong wind or heavy rain brings down a lot more. Raking them is the only solution for me now, but I would love a very large vacuum cleaner for removing them more quickly.

Does anyone have a use for gumballs? I've thought of putting up a sign that says, "Gumballs, a penny a gumball", but then I don't want to pay to have them removed, especially since I can rake them. There must be some clever people with good ideas for using gumballs. Perhaps holidays are occasions where one can use their creativity on gumballs. People make wreaths and garlands, and decorations with flowers. Thanksgiving and Christmas may provide opportunities for creative decoration formed with gumballs. The gumballs are brown but can be spray-painted for the occasion.

When I was growing up, our yard had a grove of seven gumball trees. Removing the gumballs was an annual affair. When I got married, one of the questions we should have asked was, "Are there any gumball trees on the property? " We didn't ask the question, and the house that we bought has more gumball trees than I had growing up. Should we sell this house and buy another one, there will be several things that we will consider. And the first thing will be – NO MORE GUMBALL TREES!

COURAGE

What is courage? It is not something that you can purchase at a store. When someone gives you a birthday present, that present would not be courage. Parents cannot transfer courage to their children through their genes, nor bequeath courage to their children in their wills. Courage cannot be touched, tasted, or smelled. To recognize courage, it must be seen in action.

When the odds are against you, when all hope appears gone, when there seems to be no way to victory, courage is needed. It is not through knowledge or wisdom that courage is exercised, but through the will. One must be willing to do this or that when bravery is needed. In a wartime situation, courage is not supplied by your superior. It is supplied to your heart as you will yourself to fight the battle.

Do you recall the name Lenny Skutnik? A blizzard in Washington, DC, on January 13, 1982, caused Air Florida Flight 90 to strike a bridge and plunge into the Potomac River. Seventy-eight people died. As a bystander, Lenny saw a woman unable to grab the rescue rings thrown from a helicopter, so he dove into the icy water and saved her life. He later said that no one else was doing it, and it was the only way. I say it was an act of courage for him to risk his life to save the woman's life.

Lenny's action points to another aspect of courage. Risk. Someone who exercises courage faces risks. It may risk a reputation or a promotion. Perhaps an eye, an arm, a leg, or even a life may be at risk. Who can forget the story of David and Goliath? A poor shepherd boy with only a sling and some pebbles defeats a giant with a sword and shield. David said, "Is there not a cause? " Though he was risking his life, the cause gave him the courage that he exercised to kill Goliath. He saw the battle as good versus evil, and he knew that he was on the good (God's) side. We need courage to defeat the evil giants in our day.

Courage does not always bring victory. Do you remember the Alamo? Over 180 men died, including Jim Bowie and Davy Crockett, defending the Alamo against the Mexicans under Santa Anna. As many as 6,000 Mexican troops fought, but it took over a week for them to overwhelm the fort and defeat the defenders. Did the defenders have courage? Certainly. Did they win the battle? No, but they saw a cause and sacrificed themselves for the cause.

I have read that there are very few years in Earth's history when there were no wars. Since civilizations began, man has remained uncivilized. Individuals fight, ethnic groups fight, and countries fight. The United States has fought numerous wars: The Civil War, World War I, World War II, The Korean War, and The Vietnam War. Our soldiers displayed courage to win the battles and gain the victories. There was a cause for each war, though sometimes the cause was not very popular.

There are other situations where courage is needed. Do you do any public speaking? Courage is needed, but confidence is your friend when you deliver a speech. You may say that courage and confidence go hand in hand. You have the courage to stand before your audience and the confidence that you will deliver a good speech.

You may not need to deliver a speech, or face a physical giant, or save someone from icy waters, but courage is needed because there are always battles to fight. The are battles in business, in government, in sports, and often in families. Courage is needed to fight or stand for the truth, regardless of the consequences. Determine the cause in your situation, develop your convictions, and don't back down. Be patient, be confident, and be courageous.

EATING OUT

Do you enjoy eating at a nice restaurant or even a fast-food joint? I enjoy eating anywhere good-tasting food is served. Eating is a necessity for everyone, but it can also be one of the daily pleasures in life. (I feel sorry for anyone with ulcers, diarrhea, acid reflux, or any condition where one cannot enjoy their meal.)

Some foods are so tasty that I can eat them every day. Eggs, blueberries, bananas, and hamburgers are some examples. Though I enjoy omelets, after reading about nutrition, I started eating boiled eggs. With boiled eggs, the whole egg is available to eat, so none is lost in the frying pan. Eggs are one of the most nutritious foods, and I like good nutrition.

Another one of my favorite foods is a hamburger. Two places where my wife and I eat hamburgers are Culver's and Steak N' Shake, both national fast-food restaurants. My usual burger at Culver's is the Double Butter Burger, while my wife enjoys the Mushroom burger. Culver's also sells a variety of delicious custards. Steak 'N Shake offers a variety of burgers that can be ordered with skinny fries. Both Culver's and Steak 'N Shake deliver your orders quickly. Culvers brings the food to your table while Steak N' Shake calls your name when your food is ready on the counter.

My wife and I enjoy steak at Longhorn's, a chain of steakhouses. We don't go often because the food is rather expensive and the wait at our local Longhorn's is rather long. When we do go, she orders the Fila Mignon while I get the Renegade. (She looks at the left side of the menu, but I see the right side.) For sides, she may get broccoli when I order a sweet potato with cinnamon and butter. We both enjoy the delicious bread and salad.

We also enjoy fish, though we don't eat fish often. Harbor Inn is a seafood restaurant close to home that we visited several times. Flounder stuffed with crabmeat and fried flounder are two of the entries that we order there. For saltwater fish close to the ocean, Calabash is a good choice for delicious seafood. (Calabash is a small community in southeastern North Carolina.) Captain Nance's, Captain John's, and Dockside are several restaurants for satisfying your appetite for seafood. Ella's served good seafood before it burned to the ground, but it is in the process of being rebuilt.

The meats that I eat are beef, chicken, and turkey. Hamburger, beef brisket, steak, fried chicken, broiled chicken, barbecue chicken, and turkey, especially at Thanksgiving and Christmas, are on my menu. Pork barbecue, pork chops, and bacon satisfy my wife. I don't care to eat anything that comes from a pig. When we eat where the only meat is pork in some form, I eat the slaw, hushpuppies, and whatever is served with the pork. I especially like vinegar-based slaw, though all slaws taste good.

Probably our favorite family restaurant is the Harrisburg Family Restaurant in Harrisburg, North Carolina. The food is delicious, the prices are reasonable, the portions are hearty, the atmosphere is family-friendly, and the waitresses are pretty. An extensive menu has plenty of food choices. My wife may choose the roast beef or meatloaf, as I have chicken or sirloin over rice and gravy. Her sides may be lima beans and green beans, while mine are cabbage and green beans. Banana pudding is a good choice for dessert.

Eating out is an American pastime, evidenced by the number of restaurants that cover the countryside. There are many good restaurants and many good choices for meals. If the atmosphere or food is disagreeable at one restaurant, there are plenty of other places to go for food. Most of my experiences eating out have been enjoyable. I hope that your experiences will be happy ones, also.

QUOTES

Patrick Henry - I know not what course others may take, but as for me, give me liberty or give me death.

The Emperor's New Clothes - But he has no clothes on!

Crossing the Bar - I hope to see my pilot face to face when I have crossed the Bar.

Battle Hymn of the Republic - Mine eyes have seen the glory of the coming of the Lord.

Rudyard Kipling - If you can keep your head when all about you are losing theirs and blaming it on you.

Declaration of Independence - We hold these truths to be self-evident, that all men are created equal.

President John F Kennedy - Ask not what your country can do for you. Ask what you can do for your country.

President Ronald Reagan - Mr. Gorbachev, tear down this wall.

President John F Kennedy - A man may die, nations may rise and fall, but an idea lives on.

President Ronald Reagan - Trust but verify.

President George Washington - Few men have the virtue to withstand the highest bidder.

President George Washington - It is better to offer no excuse than a bad one.

President George Washington - It is impossible to reason without arriving at a Supreme Being.

President George Washington - Worry is the interest paid by those who borrow trouble.

President Thomas Jefferson - I cannot live without books.

President Thomas Jefferson - I like the dreams of the future better than the history of the past.

President Thomas Jefferson - Whenever you do a thing, act as if all the world were watching.

President Andrew Jackson - One man with courage makes a majority.

President Andrew Jackson - Disunion by force is treason.

President Andrew Jackson - The Bible is the rock on which this republic rests.

President Andrew Jackson - There are no necessary evils in government.

President Abraham Lincoln - We cannot escape history.

President Abraham Lincoln - The better part of one's life consists of his friendships.

President Abraham Lincoln - All that I am or ever hope to be, I owe to my angel mother.

President Abraham Lincoln - Whatever you are, be a good one.

President Teddy Roosevelt - Nobody cares how much you until they know how much you care.

President Teddy Roosevelt - Keep your eyes on the stars and your feet on the ground.

President Teddy Roosevelt - Do what you can, with what you have, where you are.

President Teddy Roosevelt - Speak softly and carry a big stick; you will go far.

President Teddy Roosevelt - Every immigrant who comes here should be required within 5 years to learn English or leave the country.

President Calvin Coolidge - Collecting more taxes than is absolutely necessary is legalized robbery.

President Calvin Coolidge - The nation that forgets to defend itself will itself be forgotten.

President Calvin Coolidge - No person was ever honored for what he received.

President Calvin Coolidge - If you don't say anything, you won't be called on to repeat it.

President Herbert Hoover - Blessed are the young, for they shall inherit the national debt.

President Herbert Hoover - The budget should be balanced not by more taxes but by reduction of follies.

President Herbert Hoover - No public man can be just a little crooked.

President Herbert Hoover - It is just as important that business keep out of government as that government keep out of business.

Ralph Waldo Emerson - Life is a journey, not a destination.

Mark Twain - Actions speak louder than words.

Friedrich Nietzsche - What doesn't kill you makes you stronger

Oscar Wilde – Be yourself – Everyone else is already taken.

RIGHT OR WRONG

What is right and what is wrong? What determines if a matter is right or wrong? Do these moral choices apply to animals as well as to people? Knowing what is right and what is wrong is very important, so let's consider this matter.

My dictionary offers fifty definitions for "right" but only fifteen for "wrong"(It also offers more definitions for "good" than for "bad".)That suggests that it is better to be right than to be wrong. It is certainly easier to be wrong than to be right. There are many more opportunities to be wrong. Think of a test where one question is "What is the capital of Japan? " The only right answer is Tokyo, while there could be a myriad number of wrong answers.

Think of a society with laws. Laws help determine what is right and what is wrong for a society. Without laws, there is anarchy; anything goes, and what is right for me may be wrong for you. Laws are made to make society livable. Good laws protect the innocent from the guilty, make restitution for damages suffered, and form patterns of life for people to live. Consider traffic laws, health laws, and regulations for business. Bad laws may be made without foresight or for the benefit of a select few instead of for society at large. The IRS keeps changing the tax codes so that tax loopholes benefit those who can afford them.

Can animals be right or wrong? They are not governed by laws. Where an animal is owned by someone, the laws apply to the owner. Let's say the owner owns a dog. The law may require the owner to vaccinate his dog and to leash his dog or keep him fenced to prevent him from harming someone. If the dog harms someone, the law may demand compensation for the victim. It was wrong for the dog to bite, and if the injury was severe, that dog may be put down. But the bite was not made because of right or wrong, but from instinct. (Or maybe the dog was having a bad day and wanted to vent his frustrations.)

Our sense of right or wrong is spiritual. The problem in the Garden of Eden was not the grape on the tree but the pair on the ground. Their decision to eat the fruit precipitated a host of thou shalts and thou shalt nots from God over thousands of years. When it was apparent that God's commands would or could not be obeyed, He wrapped His final command in one word: Love. The command that started with 'Don't eat' became 'Do love'. Now, when we decide if a thing is right or wrong, we must consider if our decision is made from an attitude of love. (We must even love our enemies!) It is so much simpler than remembering and keeping more and more commandments.

TRUE OR FALSE

I suppose the simplest way to distinguish true from false is with a test. "How many eggs are in a dozen? " The true or correct answer is twelve. Any other answer is false. (You may recall the chapter Right or Wrong where Tokyo was the right answer.). We say what is true is right and what is false is wrong, but what are the differences?

My dictionary has twenty-five definitions for true and twelve for false. You might conclude that it is more important to be true than to be false, and you are right. It's also much easier to be true. When you speak the truth, you don't need to change your story. If you speak a falsehood, a comparison with the truth will reveal that you are incorrect. You may keep changing your story until your lies catch up with you.

Being true is being honest. Your life reflects your speech, your walk, and your decisions. You hide nothing that needs to be revealed. Nothing else needs to be said, and nothing needs to be changed. As the opposite of truth, being false is being dishonest. Your language, your behavior, and your motives are an extension of your dishonesty. Eventually, you will lose credibility, so people will not believe you. Friends, a job, and relationships are all in jeopardy when lies are promoted as truth.

A distinction needs to be made between truth and right. When the answer to a question or problem is correct, the answer is true, and it is right. The difference is an issue of character. There is an honest or moral character to truth. The person who speaks truth speaks from the conviction of his heart. He is right in what he does, but it is his conviction that makes him truthful. The opposite applies to one who answers falsely. He has convictions, also, but they are not honest. His decisions have an ulterior motive, so what he says or does cannot be trusted. A lot of insight may be needed to determine the truth from falsehood.

Counterfeit bills are the false currency of a country. Crooks may print twenty-dollar bills from false plates or a computer to imitate the true currency. (If the plates are stolen, the bills would still be invalid because the bills would be printed illegally.)They plan to trick people into thinking the currency is valid so it can be introduced into circulation. Bank tellers can spot the false bills by comparing them with true bills. Any bills not appearing as true bills will be rejected.

In a court, witnesses are often used to validate the truth. Plaintiffs and defendants use witnesses to support their defense or put into question the defense's testimony. Either side may disregard the truth, using a false witness and hoping the jury or judge believes the testimony of the false witness.

Sometimes when information is presented, it is so convoluted and obfuscated that it is difficult to determine what is true and what is false. When the facts are unclear or misleading, it is vital that a witness's testimony be true. It takes a discerning judge and jury to determine the validity of a witness's testimony. The deceit of a false witness must be revealed so the truth can prevail.

SLOGANS

Be All That You Can Be. --- U. S. ARMY1981 – 2001, Revived in 2023

The Breakfast of Champions. --- WHEATIES CEREAL

Finger Lickin' Good. --- KFC (KENTUCKY FRIED CHICKEN)

Betcha Can't Eat Just One. --- LAY'S

Taste the Rainbow. --- SKITTLES

Snap, Crackle, Pop. --- RICE KRISPIES CEREAL

I'm Lovin' It. --- MCDONALD'S

Choosy Moms Choose Jif. --- JIFFY PEANUT BUTTER

Think Outside the Bun. --- TACO BELL

Have It Your Way. --- BURGER KING

Eat Fresh. --- SUBWAY

Eat Mor Chikin. --- CHICK-FIL-A

Where's the Beef? --- WENDY'S

When You're Here, You're Family. --- OLIVE GARDEN

Trix Are for Kids. --- TRIX CEREAL

Melts in your Mouth, not in your Hands. --- M & M'S

M'm M'm Good. --- CAMPBELL'S SOUP

In Sight, It Must Be Right. --- STEAK N SHAKE

Welcome to Delicious. --- CULVER'S

We Have the Meats. --- ARBY'S

YUMMM. --- RED ROBIN

Always fresh, never Frozen. --- Five Guys

Seafood with Standards. --- RED LOBSTER

No one outpizzas the Hut. --- PIZZA HUT

Oh, Yes We Did! --- DOMINO'S

One Thing any Family can agree on. --- PIZZA INN

PIZZA! PIZZA!. --- LITTLE CAESARS

Home of the Flavored Crust Pizza. --- HUNGRY HOWIES

Endless Possibilities. --- CICI'S PIZZA

A pizza you can't refuse. --- GODFATHER'S PIZZA

Life is Short, Eat Better Pizza. --- JET'S PIZZA

Better Ingredients, Better Pizza. --- PAPA JOHN'S

America Runs on Dunkin'. --- Dunkin' Donuts

NICKNAME OF STATES

Alabama –Camellia State

Alaska -The Last Frontier

Arizona -Grand Canyon State

Arkansas -Razorback State

California –Golden State

Colorado -Centennial State

Connecticut –Constitution State

Delaware –First State

Florida -Sunshine State

Georgia –Peach State

Hawaii –Aloha State

Idaho-Gem State

Illinois –Land of Lincoln

Indiana –Hoosier State

Iowa –Hawkeye State

Kansas –Sunflower State

Kentucky –Bluegrass State

Louisiana – Pelican State

Maine –Pine Tree State

Maryland –Old Line State

Massachusetts – Bay State

Michigan –Great Lakes State

Minnesota –Land of 10,000 Lakes

Mississippi –Magnolia State

Missouri –Show Me State

Montana -Big Sky State

Nebraska –Cornhusker State

Nevada –Silver State

New Hampshire –Granite State

New Jersey –Garden State

New Mexico –Land of Enchantment

New York –Empire State

North Carolina – Tar Heel State

North Dakota –Roughrider State

Ohio – The Buckeye State

Oklahoma –Sooner State

Oregon –Beaver State

Pennsylvania –Keystone State

Rhode Island –Ocean State

South Carolina – Palmetto State

South Dakota –Coyote State

Tennessee –Volunteer State

Texas –Lone Star State

Utah –Beehive State

Vermont –Green Mountain State

Virginia –Old Dominion

Washington –Evergreen State

West Virginia –Mountain State

Wisconsin –Badger State

Wyoming – Cowboy State

BASEBALL STATISTICS AND FUN FACTS

The following statistics are from the 'modern era' of baseball, which is dated from 1900.

The highest batting average in a season was . 426 by Nap Lajoie in 1901.

The highest batting average in a career was . 366 by Ty Cobb.

The most hits in a season were 262 by Ichiro Suzuki in 2004.

The most hits in a career were 4,256 by Pete Rose.

The most home runs in a season were 73 by Barry Bonds in 2001

The most home runs in a career were 762 by Barry Bonds.

The most triples in a season were 36 by Owen Wilson in 1912.

The most triples in a career were 309 by Sam Crawford.

The most doubles in a season were 67 by Earl Webb in 1831.

The most doubles in a career were 792 by Tris Speaker.

The most singles in a season were 225 by Ichiro Suzuki in 2004.

The most singles in a career were 3,215 by Pete Rose.

The most RBIs in a season were 191 by Hack Wilson in 1930.

The most RBIs in a career were 2,297 by Hank Aaron.

The most stolen bases in a season were 130 by Rickie Henderson in 1982,

The most stolen bases in a career were 1,406 by Rickie Henderson.

The most walks by a batter in a season were 232 by Barry Bonds in 2004.

The most walks by a batter in a career were 2,558 by Barry Bonds.

The most consecutive games with a hit are 56 by Joe DiMaggio in 1941.

The most consecutive games played is 2,632 by Cal Ripken, Jr. over 16 seasons.

Fernando Tatis, Sr. is the only player to hit two grand slams in one inning.

Don Baylor played on four World Series teams.

Randy Johnson once threw a pitch that killed a bird.

A ground rule triple occurs when a player tries to use his hat to stop a ball.

The first baseball rule book was issued in 1877.

Nolan Ryan had the longest career in baseball, spanning 27 years.

A team must have 90 baseballs on hand for each game.

The most wins in a season were 41 by Jack Chesbro in 1904.

The most wins in a career were 511 by Cy Young.

The lowest ERA in a season was 1. 000 by Butch Leonard in 1914.

The lowest ERA in a career was 1. 82 by Ed Walsh from 1904 through 1917.

The most strikeouts in a season were 393 by Nolan Ryan in 1973.

The most walks in a season were 208 by Bob Feller in 1938.

The most walks in a career were 2,795 by Nolan Ryan.

The most strikeouts in a career were 5,714 by Nolan Ryan.

Cy Young completed 749 complete games.

Joe Sewell struck out only 114 times in 7,132 plate appearances.

FOOTBALL STATISTICS AND FUN FACTS

The most touchdown passes by a quarterback in a game is 7 by Nick Foles in 2013.

The most touchdown passes by a quarterback in a season were 55 by Peyton Manning.

The most touchdowns by a quarterback in a season were 60 by Peyton Manning.

The most touchdown passes by a quarterback in a career were 624 by Tom Brady.

The most passing yardage in one game is 554 by Norm Van Brocklin in 1951.

The most passing yardage in a season is 5,477 by Peyton Manning in 2013.

The most passing yardage in a career is 89,214 by Tom Brady.

The most interception touchdowns in a game are 2 tied by 28 players.

The most interception touchdowns in a season are 5 by DaRon Bland in 2023.

The most career interception touchdowns are 12 by Rod Woodson.

The most interception touchdowns by a team in one game is 4 by the Seattle Seahawks.

The most interceptions thrown in a game were 8 by Jim Hardy in 1950.

The most interceptions thrown in a season were 42 by George Blanda in 1962.

The most interceptions thrown in a career were 336 by Brett Favre.

The most interceptions made in a game is 5 held by 12 players.

The most interceptions made in a season were 14 by Night Train Lane in 1952.

The most interceptions made in a career were 81 by Paul Krause.

The most touchdowns by a back in one game is 6 held by three players.

The most touchdowns by a back in a season is 28 by LaDainian Tomlinson in 2006.

The most touchdowns by a back in a career is 175 by Emmitt Smith.

The most touchdowns by a receiver in one game is 5, held by three players.

The most touchdowns by a receiver in a season is 23 by Randy Moss in 2007.

The most touchdowns by a receiver in a career is 208 by Jerry Rice.

The longest touchdown reception was 99 yards, held by 13 players.

The longest touchdown run was 99 yards, held by two players.

The longest interception return for a touchdown was 107 yards by Ed Reed in 2008.

The longest fumble return for a touchdown was 104 yards, held by two players.

The longest kickoff return for a touchdown was 109 yards by Cordarrell Patterson in 2013.

The longest punt return for a touchdown was 103 yards by Robert Bailey in 1994.

The longest missed field goal return for a touchdown was 109 yards, held by two players.

FACTS, FACTS AND MORE FACTS

A lot of 'facts' are not true. Revisionist history confirms this fact. What our grandparents learned decades ago as facts have been changed according to the political, legal, and academic climate of our generation. Much or all of this chapter is from the Internet or Alexa. If you disagree with any of what is present as 'fact', please take it up with Alexa.

One gallon of water has 76,000 drops.

The most expensive piece of jewelry is the Hope diamond.

Thirteen diamonds have been found in North Carolina since 1893.

The jaguar has the strongest bite of any large cat.

The saltwater crocodile has the strongest bite of any animal.

The inland taipan of Australia is the most venomous snake.

The male Sydney funnel web spider is the most venomous spider.

The box jellyfish is the world's most venomous animal.

The peregrine falcon is the world's fastest animal.

The cheetah is the world's fastest land animal.

The sloth is the slowest animal.

The blue whale is the largest animal.

Elephants are the largest land animals.

The pygmy shrew is the smallest land animal.

The largest city by population is Tokyo.

Jericho is both the oldest city and the city with the lowest altitude.

Chainsaws were invested as medical tools.

Human teeth are the only part of the body that cannot heal themselves.

The unicorn is the native animal of Scotland.

Venus is the only planet to spin clockwise.

Only one letter does not appear in any state name: the letter q.

Ketchup was once sold as medicine.

You can't hum if you hold your nose.

Vatican City is the world's smallest country.

Honey does not spoil.

Smells can pass through liquids.

Hot water turns into ice before cold water.

The tongue is the strongest muscle in the body.

Coca-Cola was originally green.

Centigrade and Fahrenheit intersect at – 40 degrees.

Africa is the only continent in all four hemispheres.

There are four terrestrial planets: Mercury, Venus, Earth, and Mars.

The chicken came before the egg.

WHO SHOULD COMPETE IN SPORTS

Competition can be a good thing. People compete in academics, in politics, in business, in entertainment, and in sports. When you think of people competing against each other, sports venues are often the arenas for the competition. Football, baseball, basketball, tennis, and soccer are a few sports where the goal is to win. There must be fairness in the competition for the winner to be declared a legitimate winner. In the sports mentioned above, there should be a segregation of the sexes because men would dominate the sport because they are bigger, stronger, and faster than women.

Of course, with some sports, such as shooting, men may compete against women. (Remember Annie Oakley?). A shameful part of our recent history has been biological men identifying as women to compete with biological women and win swimming events. (What do you think of men and women changing clothes at the same time in a women's locker room?). Let me give you several examples.

Riley Gaines is a swimmer, a very good swimmer. She won competitions until a man, Lia Thomas, identified as a woman and entered their swimming events. (He also entered their locker rooms!). He would win by over a body length against the women, yet when he competed against men, he wouldn't even place. To show the absurdity of it, in a race where they tied (Way to go, Riley!), he was awarded the medal. In another sporting event, tennis, the top-ranked female player, Serena Williams, said that she would lose to a male player, Andy Murray, 6-0, 6-0. In a later competition, Karsten Braasch, who was ranked 203, beat Serena and Venus Williams in an exhibition match. To be competitive in tennis, men should play men, women should play women, and a man and woman team should play against another man and woman team.

Another sport where it is obvious that men should not compete against women is soccer. A U. S. women's team lead by Heather O'Reilly, a 3-time Olympic gold medalist, and coached by Mia Hamm, lost to a men's team 12-0. The Australian women's team, ranked number five in the world, lost to a team of 15-year-old boys 7-0. A team of 15-year-old boys from Dallas defeated the U. S. Women's National Soccer Team 5-2.

Where speed and power are concerned, men will dominate women in sports. Speed and power are required in football, basketball, and baseball, so men compete against men on the highest level. (I can't see a woman trans gendering to play in these sports.). Women will be competitive against men where skill is required, such as in archery or shooting. I say where men dominate a sport, let men compete against men and women against women. Where skill is required for the sport, let them compete against each other.

For some examples where men play men, women play women, or they team up, see below.

Sports where men and women should compete separately:

Football – Requires too much power and speed for a woman. Plus, it's too brutal.

Baseball – Requires too much power and speed for a woman.

Basketball – Requires too much power and speed for a woman.

See examples above on soccer, tennis, and swimming sports where men and women can compete against each other:

Archery – Men can compete against women

Shootings – Men can compete against women.

Curling – Men can compete against women.

Darts – Men can compete against women.

Billiards – Men can compete against women.

Another idea to consider is to let the transgender male be a rabbit, that is, a pacesetter in a race. He can set the pace for the race, thereby leading the race and being in front at the end of the race. He won't be competing against women, at least not for prizes, but he will be racing with them. The winner of the event will be the woman who finishes first. She will receive the top prize, with second and third place winners being women, also. The male can have the satisfaction of finishing first, but because he isn't competing, he will receive no reward. And he should not, under any circumstances, be allowed to enter the women's locker room (or bedroom, bathroom, or any room designated strictly for women).

WHEN ENOUGH IS ENOUGH

Perhaps you have heard the expressions, 'I have had enough', 'God is enough', 'Enough is enough', and 'There is more than enough'. When all that is needed is available, there is enough. When one who can solve the problem is present, it is enough. When you have come to the end of your rope and will do no more, you might argue that enough is enough. And when there is a superabundance of whatever is provided, you have more than enough.

Much of our population today has enough. Our transportation needs, food, clothing and shelter, entertainment needs (If there is such a thing), needs for exercise, rest, travel, and leisure are met. Our bodily needs are or can be largely satisfied. After a big meal, we may be offered a dessert, but we decline it because the meal satisfied us. During a period of exercise, we may cease early due to pain or exhaustion. A vacation may be cut short due to boredom. There has been enough food, enough exercise, and enough leisure for us to say that we have had enough.

Sometimes we cannot get enough. There are times when our needs are not met. A job is lost, a debilitating illness occurs, or hours are reduced so that there is not enough money for food, clothing, and shelter, for the basic needs of life. A relative, a friend, a church, or a local philanthropic organization may help fulfill those needs. If the needs are too great, we may realize it is out of our hands. Then we decide that God is enough to meet those needs. We realize that we must look to Him for our welfare and recovery. There is an expression that says,' When we are flat on our backs, we can only look up. '

Satisfaction is a pleasure we enjoy at mealtimes, in sports (especially when we win), in family or friendly get-togethers, and on vacations. Our favorite meals, carefully cooked to perfection and enjoyed with others, can be very satisfying. Playing a sport in which we are competitive can be challenging and rewarding in victory. A picnic, a staycation, attending a sporting event, and visiting a museum are opportunities to refresh our spirits in the company of others. When our health is good and the weather cooperates, we can enjoy these activities.

Circumstances, however, may intervene to make these events unenjoyable. Your favorite steak may be burnt, your favorite team loses in the playoffs, or your vacation plans were cancelled due to illness or injury. These events would be frustrating and upsetting. If they cascade one after the other, you may throw up your hands and say something better left unsaid. Or you may vent your frustration and exclaim, 'Enough is enough!'

Finally, there are times when everything is clicking. The baby is well-fed and resting, all the guests that have been invited to the party are present, the food is prepared, and the steaks' aroma is wafting tantalizingly through the air. There is plenty of food, more than sufficient for everyone. When an unexpected friend drops by and apologizes for interrupting, you invite them to the party. If they act guilty for not contributing any food, you can tell them, 'There is more than enough. 'In times when we have more than enough, we need to share our bounty with others.

CHARACTER DEVELOPMENT

Are you a builder or a destroyer? Do you build up or tear down? Both kinds of people inhabit our society. When it concerns buildings, walls, and old things that have outlived their usefulness, both kinds of individuals are needed. Schools, churches, apartments, roads, bridges, and all sorts of buildings are built by those with the skills and experience to do the work. These same construction works may be torn down or refurbished when they are outdated and need to be replaced. People build them and people remove them.

Because shelters are needed in our society, it is necessary that houses, apartments, and condos be built for people to inhabit. (There are not enough caves for everyone, and who wants to live in a cave!)Architects provide the blueprints to be followed. Carpenters and bricklayers sawed the wood, hammered the nails, and poured the cement used for the building. Gophers (like me) do the grunt work, like carrying tools to where they are needed. Cooperation is a requisite for a successful project.

Churches, houses, and apartments are important, but it is more important how we build our lives. There are many hindrances, many obstacles to building a life that adds to a good society. As good cement must be prepared for laying bricks, so each person needs a good education (not necessarily college). As bricklayers apply the cement to bricks, so people must apply wisdom to what they have learned. Society depends upon people with good character, and good character cannot be bought. Character is developed over time through choices that are made. Good choices can build up good character, while bad choices can tear it down. Choices must not be made flippantly but must be made with care. Education and choices are just two factors that affect character.

As lives are built, the people that we meet will affect our behavior. People in our neighborhoods, our schools, our churches, and our jobs may influence us either positively or negatively. Building a good rapport with neighbors, teachers, churchgoers, and coworkers would be helpful when disagreements arise. A good character commands respect, so that your side of any argument would be considered. A discerning mind would decide whether to pursue a matter or let the matter drop. Sometimes it is best to let the other side have their way, especially if tempers are flaring up. However, if the situation is too volatile, it may be necessary to fight until a final decision is made.

Our influence on others must be considered, especially on our children. A child's character will be affected by what they see in their parents. If the parents quarrel, the children may quarrel; if the parents curse, the children may curse; if the parents drink, the children may learn to drink. Parents are responsible for their children's development, so they must be careful to exhibit good character around their children. The parents' influence may not be enough to bring about good character in their children, but they must do all they can toward that end. The children will soon be adults, having their influence in society. The parents must work hard on character development to ensure that their influence is a good one.

MENTAL BLOCK

Exercise is a daily requirement for everyone. People need food to feed muscles and exercise to work them every day. Proper food and exercise, along with sufficient sleep, combine to provide bodies with the health needed to enjoy life and contribute to others. When too much food or the wrong kinds or combinations of food are consumed, bodies can suffer. Stomach aches, diarrhea, or constipation can result, affecting the exercise regimen. Insufficient fluids or foods may cause leg pain when exercising. A leg cramp could be the result.

Cramps in the legs and other body parts may be caused by exercise. Another type of cramp may result from mental exercise. This type of 'cramp' may be described as mental block or brain fog. Journalists, novelists, poets, and other writers often experience mental blocks. (I've been experiencing one for days.)Stretching their minds to find the right words or the right sentences to express their ideas, their minds may go blank. Halfway through a news story, a novel, or a poem, their thought processing has stopped. The idea train has left the station without them. It's then time to take a mental break and regroup.

What can be done to get back on track? One suggestion is to keep writing. Don't stop what you are doing even if the creative juices have dried up. Eventually, they should start flowing again so you can finish your article or book. A lot of irrelevant or extraneous words may need to be deleted, but that should be expected. Don't expect the piece to be complete at the first writing.

Another aid to writing is sufficient sleep. Writing requires a lot of concentration, and mental fatigue from lack of sleep affects your focus. Your body needs regular rest times to renew itself and recover from each day's activities. Thinking to find the right word or phrase requires work, and that work can be tiring. Your mind needs to recover, along with your body, so that you will have the energy to continue writing.

Sometimes it is helpful to get away, to read a book, to take a trip, to do something to take your mind off your writing. The book or trip may provide the stimulus needed to start again. Activities that you enjoy may help your mind relax, refocus, and regain the drive that will allow you to complete your work. They might help you get past the burnout that came from mental exhaustion.

Perhaps a friend, neighbor, or spouse can listen to your ideas, words, and sentences and offer suggestions. Their encouragement will give you the confidence to overcome a mental block. Your mind may be led in another direction as you respond to their suggestions. The final material may not be what you originally envisioned, but it could be better. Two heads are better than one, and if your friends are pleased with the final writing, your readers probably will be, too.

YOUR BEST FRIEND

You are familiar with the phrase, 'A dog is a man's best friend'. (Marilyn Monroe sang 'Diamonds Are a Girl's Best Friend'– maybe she never had a dog.)Dogs can be good friends if they are treated well. They are faithful, obedient, and loving to their owners. Walking them, playing games (frisbee, catch, hide and seek) with them, taking them on trips, or sitting with them in the yard or on the couch are a few activities for building a bond with your dog.

Some big dog breeds include German Shepherd, Bullmastiff, Kangal Shepherd Dog, Doberman Pincher, and Rottweiler. These and other dogs should be carefully trained so they can be a benefit to their owners and not be a danger to others. With proper training and plenty of love, they will be faithful and can accept strangers - carefully. (My experience is that Dobermans are the most unpredictable.)

Smaller dog breeds that will do well with families include Labrador Retriever, Golden Retriever, English Setter, and Irish Setter. All dogs need to be exercised, but the English Setter needs to run. Have a large yard or place where he can expend his energy. It would help if you were a runner, too.

If you would like a dog that's full of energy all the time, consider a Border Collie, Jack Russell Terrier, or a Dalmatian. These dogs define energy. They are the Energizer Dogs. Don't try to keep up with them, just let them enjoy the freedom to go, go, go. Train them well, but realize that all the training available will not affect their energy. These breeds are not for everyone, so use wisdom in deciding whether one should be your pet.

Many stories have been written about dogs. In 1906, Jack London wrote White Fang, a story about a wolf-dog hybrid in the Yukon and

Northwest Territories. He also wrote Call of the Wild, the story of a domesticated dog named Buck that became wild in the Yukon. Cujo is a novel by Stephen King about a rabid Saint Bernard named Cujo that keeps a mother and son trapped in a car. Of course, White Fang, Buck (after turning wild), and Cujo are not your typical dogs that you would consider man's best friend.

A movie that illustrates a boy's love for his dog is Old Yeller. If you haven't seen the movie, please check it out, but make sure that you have some tissues handy. It is a tearjerker. The story is that a lost dog shows up on a Texas ranch where a woman and her two sons live. One of the sons becomes very attached to the dog and has several adventures with him. When Old Yeller fights off a rabid wolf, the mother gets concerned that Old Yeller could become rabid, so Old Yeller is locked up. After a few days, he shows evidence of being rabid, so the son must shoot Old Yeller. (I get choked up just thinking about it.)

A dog can be a good companion. He can be a good friend, but be careful not to get too attached to him. Dogs don't live as long as people, so someday you may need to have your dog put down, like Old Yeller. It could be traumatic to you, because your dog is not just your friend. He is part of your family.

LOSING YOUR BEST FRIEND

Your best friend could be a parent, neighbor, schoolmate, or relative. He or she could be a man or woman, boy or girl, young or old. It may be a person or, as shown in a previous chapter, it may be a pet. In this chapter, I'm talking about pets that I had with my family and later a pet I had with my wife.

As I grew up, my family had dogs as pets. Our snake-finding dog was Duchess, a dachshund. I was a preteen when she cornered a water moccasin and discovered a corn snake. Bill, our English Setter, was a runner. He loved the Great Outdoors and loved to enjoy it by running. After going missing, he was found dead in a neighbor's yard. (I don't recall what happened to Duchess.)In my teenage years, Tiny was our family dog. As his name suggests, he was tiny because he was a chihuahua mix. One night, I let him outside (to pee?) and he never came back. My brother learned that he had fallen into a gutter around the corner from our house and wound up at the animal shelter, where he died.

After high school, I never had another pet; no dog, no cat, no animal of any kind until my second marriage. I had no pet while in college or during those years that I was single and satisfied. Having grown up with dogs, it would have been easy to have a dog in my first marriage. My first wife did not grow up with pets, so we never had to decide about getting a pet. We had each other. When she died, my life became single and satisfied again.

I wasn't looking to get married again. Sincerely, I was satisfied with living my life. Circumstances changed my focus, and after five years, I remarried. There was one caveat. My second wife had a dog, and to marry her, the dog had to come along. It was a package deal. No dog, no marriage. That was fine with me. My wife loved me, and the dog, Joey, learned to like me, and I grew attached to him.

Joey was a mixed breed. We never learned his ancestry, though I'm convinced that he was part Jack Russell. He was white dynamite, with twelve pounds of pure energy. My wife picked him up from the shelter when he was about two years old, and he was about twelve when we married. He had been attacked by larger dogs and became extremely attached to my wife. She walked him daily, a habit that I joined when we married.

Walking was an obsession with Joey. He would not rest or leave us alone until he walked. Around neighborhoods and apartment buildings, in parks, and at the lake were a few places where we walked. Meeting people was fine with Joey, especially meeting children. People commented about Joey being such a good-looking dog. Meeting dogs was not always fine. Small dogs were usually okay, if they weren't too lively. They would sniff and smell each other, then go on their ways. Joey would lunge and bark at large dogs since that was his method for defending himself from attacks.

Joey enjoyed traveling with us on trips. We might go to the beach or the lake with him resting on my wife's lap as I drove the car. On our last trip to the beach, it was obvious that Joey had a problem. The limp that he had was more noticeable there. Over several months, it became progressively worse. His eyesight and hearing had been deteriorating for some time, and now he was no longer jumping up on the couch. Though he limped, he still had wanderlust and was sent to the animal shelter after leaving the yard. When my wife and I picked him up, it was then obvious that a tough decision had to be made.

What do you do when a family member gets deathly sick? You do what you can to get them well. What do you do when a pet has lost all quality of life? We had to make that decision about Joey and …. we decided to put him down. My wife and I were in the room as they laid Joey on the table and gave him the shots. I remember the vet monitoring his heart … and saying it had stopped…. I cried and cried. (I'm crying now.)

Joey is gone. He will be missed. My wife and I now need to make another decision. Do we want another pet. It's tough losing a part of one's family, and I'm not sure that we are willing to endure that heartache again.

SOME SILLY STATE STATUTES

There are many laws on the books of our fifty states. Most are probably needed, but some, especially some old statutes, are outdated and may elicit a chuckle or two for being absurd. The following are laws from all fifty states, one from each state. Many may not be enforced now, but be careful not to violate them.

Alabama – It's illegal to put an ice cream cone in your back pocket.

Alaska – Feeding alcohol to a moose is illegal.

Arizona – It's illegal for a donkey to sleep in a bathtub after 7 pm.

Arkansas – It's illegal for a man to beat his wife more than once a month.

California – It's illegal to whistle for a canary before 7 am.

Colorado – It's illegal to keep a couch on your porch.

Connecticut – It's illegal to walk backward at night.

Delaware – Dog hair cannot be sold legally.

Florida – It's illegal for unmarried women to parachute on Sundays.

Georgia – It's illegal to live more than 90 days in a calendar year on a boat.

Hawaii – Placing a coin in one's ear is illegal.

Idaho – It is illegal to fish from a camel or giraffe.

Illinois – Giving a lit cigarette to a cat or dog is illegal.

Indiana – No horse can be driven at a speed of more than 10 mph.

Iowa – For a mustached man to kiss a woman in public is illegal.

Kansas – Whale hunting is prohibited.

Kentucky – A woman cannot marry the same man more than three times.

Louisiana – Sending an unwelcome pizza is considered harassment.

Maine – Driving barefoot is illegal.

Maryland – Buying drinks for female bartenders is illegal.

Massachusetts – You must be certified to tell fortunes.

Michigan – Motor vehicles cannot be sold, traded, or bought on Sunday.

Minnesota – Bathtubs in Minnesota must have feet.

Mississippi – Cat meat cannot be sold.

Missouri – Bear wrestling is not allowed.

Montana – Lassoing a fish is illegal.

Nebraska – If you have a venereal disease, you cannot get married.

Nevada – It is illegal to ride a camel on the highway.

New Hampshire – Collecting seaweed off the beach at night is illegal.

New Jersey – It is illegal to pump your own gas.

New Mexico – Idiots are banned from voting.

New York – Slippers cannot be worn in public places after 10 pm.

North Carolina – Singing off-key in public places is illegal.

North Dakota – Fireworks are banned after 11 pm.

Ohio – It is against the law to get a fish drunk.

Oklahoma – Don't make faces at a dog, or you may be fined.

Oregon – Do not lift weights while driving.

Pennsylvania – Being paid for fortune telling or tarot card reading is illegal.

Rhode Island – Racing a horse on a public highway is prohibited.

South Carolina – Playing pinball as a minor is illegal.

South Dakota – It's illegal to sleep in a cheese factory.

Tennessee – Selling hollow logs is not legal.

Texas – It is illegal to eat your neighbor's garbage (unless you have their permission).

Utah – Causing a catastrophe is illegal.

Vermont – A husband must give his approval for his wife to wear false teeth,

Virginia – You cannot have a skunk as a pet.

Washington – Don't sleep in someone else's outhouse without permission.

West Virginia – It's illegal to whistle underwater.

Wisconsin – You must not tease a skunk.

Wyoming – Women must not be standing within five feet of a bar while drinking.